SAM SHEPARD

LITERATURE AND LIFE: AMERICAN WRITERS

Select list of titles in the series:

Louis Auchincloss	*Christopher C. Dahl*
Saul Bellow	*Robert F. Kiernan*
Truman Capote	*Helen S. Garson*
James Fenimore Cooper	*Robert Emmet Long*
Stephen Crane	*Bettina L. Knapp*
Emily Dickinson	*Bettina L. Knapp*
E. L. Doctorow	*John G. Parks*
Theodore Dreiser	*James Lundquist*
Robert Frost	*Elaine Barry*
Nathaniel Hawthorne	*Edward Wagenknecht*
Joseph Heller	*Judith Ruderman*
Ernest Hemingway	*Peter L. Hays*
The Novels of Henry James	*Edward Wagenknecht*
The Tales of Henry James	*Edward Wagenknecht*
Jack London	*James Lundquist*
Henry Wadsworth Longfellow	*Edward Wagenknecht*
Mary McCarthy	*Willene Schaefer Hardy*
H. L. Mencken	*Vincent Fitzpatrick*
James A. Michener	*George J. Becker*
Arthur Miller	*June Schlueter and James K. Flanagan*
Henry Miller	*J. D. Brown*
Anaïs Nin	*Bettina L. Knapp*
Clifford Odets	*Gabriel Miller*
John O'Hara	*Robert Emmet Long*
The Plays of Eugene O'Neill	*Virginia Floyd*
Edgar Allan Poe	*Bettina L. Knapp*
J. D. Salinger	*James Lundquist*
Gertrude Stein	*Bettina L. Knapp*
John Steinbeck	*Paul McCarthy*
William Styron	*Judith Ruderman*
James Thurber	*Robert Emmet Long*
Mark Twain	*Robert Keith Miller*
Nathanael West	*Robert Emmet Long*
Thornton Wilder	*David Castronovo*
Edmund Wilson	*David Castronovo*

Complete list of titles in the series available from the publisher on request.

SAM SHEPARD

Martin Tucker

A Frederick Ungar Book
CONTINUUM · NEW YORK

1992

The Continuum Publishing Company
370 Lexington Avenue, New York, NY 10017

Printed in the United States of America

Library of Congress Cataloging-in-Publication Data

Tucker, Martin.
Sam Shepard / Martin Tucker.
p. cm. — (Literature and life. American writers)
"A Frederick Ungar book."
Includes bibliographical references and index.
ISBN 0-8264-0549-5
1. Shepard, Sam, 1943– . 2. Dramatists, American—20th century—Biography. I. Title. II. Series.
PS3569.H394Z92 1992
812′.54—dc20 91-15805
[B] CIP

Contents

Preface: Sam Shepard and His Plays

This book is about Sam Shepard's plays. Biography is noted, particularly in its relevance to Shepard's treatment of imagistic detail. Shepard's two books of prose and poems, *Hawk Moon* and *Motel Chronicles,* are given attention, and his journal, *Rolling Thunder Logbook,* is acknowledged. The spine of this book remains, however, in its overview of Shepard's extraordinary dramatic work, and analyses of Shepard's first play through *A Lie of the Mind* are provided for clues to Shepard's attitudes to events around him and to those events that have shaped his life. The analyses are presented in chronological order, that is, according to the historical dates of first production; where composition significantly precedes production, notice is given to the reader.

This study does not make a claim for a literal connection between the work and Shepard's life, but it suggests that Shepard's work is the truest source for discovery of his humanistic view of worldly ironies and for his sense of apprehension of the roles that his literal family and his family of man have played in his life. Thus, particular attention is paid to recurrence of imagery, the recurrence signifying to the writer of this study a stream of subconsciousness that reveals more than it tells under its order of formally chartered exploration. With some few exceptions, brief biographical data precedes the analyses for the sake of a comprehensive and transitional approach to an artist's achievement. The opening and the second chapter provide general statements about Shepard's career and his early experiences as a member of his family and of the community of his high school days, both of which orders of experience reverberate in his work. The final chapter provides a series of "notes"—together they form a field of commentary on aspects of Shepard and his work that continue to reveal and to mystify. Both the man, Samuel Shepard Rogers III, and his plays, written under the name Sam Shepard, tease the reader/audience into making discoveries and connections between the facts given and the clues suggested, but the final script refuses to resolve the mysteries and paradoxes presented. The technique is not unfamiliar in life or in the history of literary art. It is as effective (and when uneffective as frustratingly annoying) as an artist has it in his power to make it so. The last chapter suggests a connection with Shepard's work—in its provocation of argument for the irresolute as a ticket to a newer and further journey—with Shepard's attitude to the public attention paid him.

As this book was going to press, an announcement appeared in the *New York Times* on March 15, 1991, which stated that a production of a new Shepard play, *States of Shock,* was to open on April 26, 1991, at the American Place Theatre. The popular film and stage actor, John Malkovich, was to star in Shepard's first new play in five years, and Bill Hart, an old friend from his first years in New York (Shepard shared an apartment with him in 1967), was to direct it. The *Times* piece noted that the play had five characters and was set in a small family restaurant; no other information was "available."

Shepard's decision to keep confidential anything relating to the production or to his own script until opening night is not without precedent. Indeed, it is reminiscent of his behavior with *La Turista* and with many of his later plays. It reflects both a fear of distraction by hostile and/or misunderstanding detractors; it represents as well a decision to present the work to the public only when formally unveiled. In so doing, Shepard reveals a complex of ambivalences: he urges spontaneity in his work and the gesture of openness in the processes of understanding conflict, and yet he exhibits a demand for control, a control that intrudes into the presence of his work arena. Such control—or desire for it—and the concomitant taking of action to achieve it produces an extraordinary tension in Shepard's work. It weaves a texture of paradox in his dramas.

Because of the limitations of deadline for this book, Shepard's new work could not be included in the text for analysis. It is, however, fully reviewed in the appendix.

In lieu of endnotes, sources for all references may be found in the bibliography.

Chronology

1943	Born November 5, in Fort Sheridan, Illinois, an army base near Chicago, to Jane Elaine Schook Rogers and Samuel Shepard Rogers. Oldest of three children (two sisters); named Samuel Shepard Rogers III.
1944–55	Shepard spends childhood as an "army brat" on various bases from South Dakota to Florida to Utah to Guam.
1955	Father leaves army, moves family to California; Shepard spends high-school years in Duarte.
1961	Shepard graduates from high school, attends three semesters of a junior college in northern California.
1962	Shepard joins the Bishop's Company Repertory Players, goes on cross-country tour with group.
1963	Shepard leaves theatrical repertory group in New York, and moves into East Village apartment of old Duarte pal, Charlie Mingus, Jr. Shepard works as waiter/busboy in the Village Gate and Marie's Crisis Cafe. Meets Ralph Cook, founder of Theater Genesis.
1964	Samuel Shepard Rogers III changes name to Sam Shepard. *Cowboys* and *Rock Garden,* his first plays, produced at Theater Genesis on October 10, 1964.
1965–66	Shepard claims drug addiction at draft board examination. Shepard meets actress Joyce Aaron; the two live together for two years. Shepard and Aaron take vacation trip to Mexico; the experience will prove inspiration for *La Turista.* Shepard will vow never to fly again as result of airplane trip in Mexico. Several of his one-act plays produced off-off-Broadway. Shepard awarded Obies for *Chicago, Icarus's Mother,* and *Red Cross.*

1967 Shepard is awarded Rockefeller Foundation grant. *La Turista,* his first two-act play, produced. *Melodrama Play* presented at La Mama ETC. *Cowboys No. 2* receives premiere at Mark Taper Forum in Los Angeles, later appears in New York under direction of Bill Hart; produced in London in 1972. *Forensic and the Navigators* produced by Theater Genesis.

1968 Shepard receives Guggenheim Foundation grant. Shepard collaborates on film script of *Me and My Brother* for director Robert Frank. Shepard journeys to Rome to write *Zabriskie Point* for director Michelangelo Antonioni; script is not used. Shepard works in England on *Maxagasm,* a film project for the Rolling Stones musical group; film is not made.

1969 Shepard marries O-lan Johnson. *The Holy Ghostly* presented on La Mama European tour. *The Unseen Hand* produced at La Mama ETC.

1970 Shepard's first son Jesse Mojo born. *Operation Sidewinder* opens at Vivian Beaumont Theatre in Lincoln Center. First version of script was written in 1969 and scheduled for Yale Repertory Theatre, but protests by black students led Shepard to withdraw the production. *Shaved Splits,* a one-act play, is presented at La Mama ETC in July. Shepard appears in movie *Brand X,* directed by Win Chamberlin.

1971 *Mad Dog Blues* produced at Theater Genesis. *Back Bog Beast Bait* produced at American Place Theatre. *Cowboy Mouth* first presented at Traverse Theatre in Edinburgh; later produced in New York with Shepard and Patti Smith as the two leads. Shepard and wife O-lan separate; he moves into Smith's apartment; Shepard returns to wife. Departs for self-exile in England with wife and son.

1972 *The Tooth of Crime* premieres in London at Open Space Theatre.

1973 *Hawk Moon,* a collection of stories, poems, and monologues, published by Black Sparrow Press, Los Angeles.

1973 *Blue Bitch* filmed for BBC Television. American production, directed by Murray Mednick, by Theater Genesis. *The Tooth of Crime* receives first production at McCarter Theater, Princeton University. Richard Schechner directs a new, and controversial, production for Performance Group. This "environmental" production is filmed for Whitney Museum, New York. *Nightwalk,* a "collective work" written with Jean-Claude van Itallie and Megan Terry as part of Open Theatre project, presented at St. Clement's Church, New York, on September 8.

1974 *Geography of a Horse Dreamer* produced at Royal Court Theatre in London. Produced in New York at Manhattan Theatre Club. *Little Ocean,* a one-act play about pregnancy, produced at Hampstead Theatre Club in London. No American production. Shepard returns to US with his family. After a short stay at his Nova Scotia farm, he moves family to California.

1975 Shepard is hired as screenwriter for Bob Dylan's Rolling Thunder Revue. Shepard keeps journal of the tour, which is published as *Rolling Thunder Logbook. Action,* written in England, produced at American Place Theatre in New York, in a double bill with the monologue-play, *Killer's Head,* in which Richard Gere plays a man about to be electrocuted.

1976 Shepard receives a fifteen-thousand-dollar Rockefeller grant. He is awarded a Brandeis University Creative Arts Medal. Shepard joins Magic Theatre Company in San Francisco as participating playwright. *Angel City* produced at Magic Theatre. *Suicide in B♭* produced at Yale Repertory Theatre, New Haven. *The Sad Lament of Pecos Bill on the Eve of Killing His Wife,* a music drama (all roles are sung), is presented at Bay Area Playwrights Festival in San Francisco. *Inacoma,* an improvisatory drama coordinated by Shepard is produced at Magic Theatre.

1977 *Curse of the Starving Class,* Shepard's first produced three-act play, receives premiere at Royal Court Theatre in London; American production is at Joseph Papp's

New York Shakespeare Festival, Public Theater. *Rolling Thunder Logbook* published by Viking Press.

1978 *Seduced* presented at Trinity Square Repertory Company, Providence, Rhode Island. New York production at American Place Theatre. *Tongues,* a collaboration with Joseph Chaikin, produced at Magic Theatre. Shepard appears briefly in *Renaldo and Clara,* written and directed by Bob Dylan. Director Terrence Malick, seeing clips, selects Shepard to play lead in *Days of Heaven* with Richard Gere and Brooke Adams.

1979 *Savage/Love,* a companion piece to *Tongues* written in collaboration with Joseph Chaikin, produced in double bill with *Tongues* at Joseph Papp's Public Theater. *Buried Child* presented first at Magic Theatre in San Francisco. New York production at the Theater for the New City; production later moved to commercial run at Theatre de Lys in New York. *Jacaranda,* a text for a dance drama performed by Daniel Nagrin.

1980 *True West* produced at Magic Theatre; moves to New York at Joseph Papp's Shakespeare Festival, Public Theater. Director Robert Woodruff and Papp quarrel over staging; Papp replaces Woodruff. Shepard plays lead in film, *Resurrection,* with Ellen Burstyn as co-star.

1981 *Superstitions,* drawn from material in what will be published as *Motel Chronicles,* is presented under a pseudonym, Walker Hayes. Shepard's wife O-lan is in the cast. Appears in film *Raggedy Man,* directed by Jack Fisk, with Sissy Spacek and Eric Roberts. Shepard meets Jessica Lange on set of *Frances.*

1982 *Frances,* directed by Graeme Clifford, released for distribution. *Motel Chronicles,* with photographs, is published by City Lights Books, San Francisco. A collection of prose poems, poems, monologues, and dream visions, it is dedicated to Shepard's mother.

1983 Shepard's father dies as result of car accident on highway. Shepard and wife divorce. He and Jessica Lange buy ranch near Santa Fe, New Mexico, and live there with their children for five years. Shepard receives Academy Award nomination for role in *The Right Stuff,* directed by Philip Kaufman, in which he plays astronaut Chuck Yeager. *Fool for Love* produced at Magic Theatre. Production brought to New York, where it has long run at Circle Repertory Company. Shepard writes script for film version directed by Robert Altman and in which he costars with Kim Basinger.

1984 *Paris, Texas,* based on Shepard's *Motel Chronicles,* is produced and released. Shepard wrote screenplay, and Wim Wenders directed film which won Palme d'Or at Cannes Film Festival. Shepard teaches a playwriting course in Cambridge, Massachusetts. Shepard and Joseph Chaikin write a radio play, *The War in Heaven.* A monologue, it is performed by Chaikin, with music by Shepard, on WBAI Radio, New York. *Country,* in which he costars with Jessica Lange, is released.

1985 *A Lie of the Mind* premieres at Promenade Theatre, New York, on December 5.

1986–90 Shepard and Jessica Lange become parents of their first child, a daughter, Hannah, in 1986. A year later (1987), a second child, their son Samuel, is born to them. Shepard and Lange buy a horse farm/ranch in Orange County, Virginia. It becomes their main home and children go to school there. Shepard acts and directs in several movies for which he wrote the screenplays as well. Other projects include *Crimes of the Heart* (1987), in which both he and Jessica Lange starred, and *Last Call for Passenger Faber,* based on a novel by Max Frisch, and filmed in Vera Cruz, Mexico, in spring of 1990. Shepard publishes a one-act play, *True Dylan,* in *Esquire.*

1991 Shepard's play *States of Shock* begins performances at American Place Theatre, New York on April 30.

1

Introduction

Sam Shepard's work has been a movement from the middle of a situation back to its beginning. All his work is, in one sense, a journey to the beginning of something in order that he or his characters can start moving into the venue from which they started; by moving back, they begin moving out and forward again. Their journey is not so much a journey outward—in the beginning of his writing career it was never a journey inward—but rather a manipulation through which he pilots characters into some groping for the first moment of growth, the initiation of awareness of their situations. The moment, and the movements toward it, are tentative, and Shepard avoids all the easy (and, it should be added, some of the difficult) techniques and rationalizations of behavioristic psychology and naturalistic logic in his ensuing dramatic treatments. Ultimately he comes down on the side of the manic monologue, an outpouring by a character in which reigning emotions and desires are put forth in a dazzling self-centeredness. This manic monologue does not resolve the dramatic situation, but it puts it in a new light or sense of its "place." From this point the beginning of insight follows; from this point the play announces its initiation of the drama that must follow beyond the physical confines of the theater. Shepard's sense of the importance of this kind of "place" can be seen in all his plays, and even in the title of the works—compare *Chicago; La Turista; True West,* among others.

Shepard does not plan his work in this manner. Indeed, his statements on his craft and/or his writing suggest he is an artist who denies self-consciousness. Yet it is a justifiable position that Shepard has a sense of what he is doing and a real sense of where he is going. In examining his work, and in following its sequence, a reader/viewer can see the good Shepard on a pilgrimage to the starting point of a journey. Curiously, Shepard seems to stop at the starting point once he has reached it. *A Lie of the Mind,* his most extensive treatment of themes invidious through his writing up to that play, left Shepard in a six-year quandary with his writing, unable to move forward, or, to his credit, unable to repeat his themes without a new approach to them. He was apparently working on play and film scripts without finishing any of them. Shepard's behavior is familiar in this regard—he is famous for his proclaimed dislike of "endings" or resolutions. Whether his view is a rationalized argument of personal defense or an objectified critical stance, his statements on "endings" denounce closure as a vitiation of the spontaneous spirit.

Shepard was also working as an actor in several films during this period, and occasionally as a director; in 1989–90 he increased his one-film-a-year commitment to three major roles. The six-year gestation period between *A Lie of the Mind* and his only since-produced play confirms that Shepard has completed an initial phase in his career and rounded out a field he has honed to perfection. Where he will go is another matter, and one not clear from what has gone before in his work, but where he has been is becoming increasingly clearer, and the patterns that have shaped his creative passions can now be apprehended without dismembering the limberness of his fleet-footed, indivisible dramatic creations. Such patterns suggest that Shepard, far from writing off the top of his head (or on the backs of Tootsie Roll wrappers, as his onetime companion Patti Smith claimed in *Sam Shepard: 9 Random Years*) was writing from the bottom of his psyche. This psychic sediment accounts for his irony, and sometimes savagery; it accounts for his unique twists of the lens of a viewpoint. It does not account for Shepard's genius, but it is the agent through which that genius manifests itself.

Sam Shepard's star surfaced on the off-Broadway theater scene in the early 1960s. He had been living in New York City's Lower East Side with his Duarte, California, high school pal, Charles Mingus, Jr. Working as a busboy along with Mingus (Mingus had got him the job) at Greenwich Village's folksong-jazz nightclub-eatery, Art D'Lugoff's Village Gate, Shepard befriended the headwaiter there, Ralph Cook. Cook had recently founded his own dramatic company, Theater Genesis; he agreed to put on two of Shepard's plays. Cook's production proved the genesis of Shepard's playwriting career, for although the plays were given negative notices or a deafening absence of critical commentary, they attracted the notice of the *Village Voice* reviewer, Michael Smith. Smith was not sure of the meaning of what he saw, but he was positive about the presence of Shepard's vitality. His favorable review in the most important alternative newspaper of the time shaped Shepard's life in that, as a result of the review and the attention it gained for Shepard, the young playwright decided to remain in New York and to continue at his playwriting career. Shepard was to live eight more years in New York City and to become the most celebrated young playwright of his time. Ironically, when he was given his chance at the big time—a production of a new play at the prestigious Vivian Beaumont Theatre in Lincoln Center—Shepard found himself in the midst of professional derailment. His ambitious new play was a failure on its first outing, and his various trysts with other big-time actitivies—a writing job with the famed Italian director Michelangelo Antonioni and another movie-writing job with the Rolling Stones—proved cataclysmic to his professional reputation and to his self-esteem. Shepard, who had fled Duarte when he was nineteen years old for a cross-country tour with a church dramatics group and disembarked in New York City, now fled his scene again. This time he left New York City for almost four years in exile in London, a period in which he underwent personal crises of identity and direction. When he returned to the United States in 1974, he avoided New York City and the East Coast for ten years, returning to Cambridge in 1984 to teach a playwriting workshop and to visit his ailing friend Joseph Chaikin in New York. (It is of some interest that Shepard's father died in 1983, a death that likely made Shepard more aware of his own mortality and the need to cross physical and psychic territories before the invasion of fatality.) He lived for several years in a house and ranch in New Mexico with Jessica Lange after the two of them met on a movie set. (Shepard had a featured role in Lange's starring film, *Frances*.) In 1988 he and Lange moved to a horse farm in the hills of Virginia, where they now live with their two children, and, sometimes, each of their two children from previous relationships. (Lange's first child, Alexandra, is the daughter of the ballet dancer-director-producer Mikhail Baryshnikov; Lange and Baryshnikov never married.) Various rumors circulate that Shepard and Lange have married, but there is no official confirmation of any union other than the fact that they have lived together for ten years and that each continues to proclaim his/her love of the other.

In the course of his career Shepard has thus moved from a loft in which waiters, busboys, and itinerant craftsmen working at menial jobs have performed on weekends to small and enthusiastic crowds to the kind of upscale treatment afforded movie icons and media celebrities. His first theatrical venture was a birth not so much planned as an opportunity conceived for an uncertain future. From that plane Shepard has soared to a level of critical acceptance as a major American playwright. He has become a movie star, a role demanding a different kind of focus from that of the creative writer. The irony is one familiar in the history of American and European drama: the rebel-bohemian of yesterday has become the theater-garden sage of a later afternoon, yet now his dramatic leaves show less-exuberant weeds of expression, less-cutting blades of growth.

Shepard is still a young man and his greatest work may yet appear: Ibsen and Yeats produced their masterpieces long after they turned sixty; Robert Frost, Eugene O'Neill, and Samuel Beckett, among others, never let age deter them from their narrative, dramatic, and lyric tasks. Whether his five-year tenure of writing silence was planned, transient, or a necessary subconscious stage in an artist's germination remains to be determined, but its fact provides evidence that a curtain has fallen on one period of the dramatist's life, that an act or stage of career has had its climax presented. The rest is the future, which Shepard, in his habits of privacy, is husbanding.

The "acts" of Shepard's "play" are interpreted in the following pages. I use the word *play* in a singular sense, for Shepard has always regarded drama as "play" from his earliest conceptions of the dramatic medium. For him "play" is not so much a written text as a situation for provocation of expression, a germ of an idea in a fever of words. In Shepard's situations, or "play," a dramatic conflict provokes both the unexpected personal reaction and an abiding mythic consciousness, both the length of a "manic monologue" and a reverberating silence in which to weave a tapestry of several threads. Above all, Shepard's "play" is comedy in his handling of it. It is the playing on, or teasing of, character foibles that produces Shepard's profoundest responses and descriptive powers. Shepard put it in this way: "The reason I began writing plays was the hope of extending the sensation of *play* (as in 'kid') on into adult life. If 'play' becomes 'labor,' why play?" ("Visualization, Language, and the Inner Library," *Drama Review,* 50).

2

The Early Days: Duarte; the Early Days in New York

"Sam Shepard" was *not* born November 5, 1943, in a hospital at Fort Sheridan, Illinois, near Chicago. Rather the eldest son of Samuel Shepard Rogers, Sr., and Jane Elaine Schook Rogers was born that day. The father was not present: he was on duty as a bomber pilot in Italy. The baby was christened Samuel Shepard Rogers III; he chose to style himself as "Steve" through his childhood and high school days. He grew up an "army brat" at various bases in Florida, South Dakota, Utah, and on the island of Guam. In his plays and in his prose-fiction and prose-poems in *Hawk Moon* and *Motel Chronicles,* Shepard alludes many times to the image of his mother with a gun at her side, protecting her family at an army air force base in Guam from Japanese snipers. Shepard recalls, in one prose-poem, riding in a jeep to see the Walt Disney movie, *Song of the South,* at an outdoor screening on the air force base. He recalls his mother with her trusty pistol near her hand; the child is aware that Japanese soldiers in hiding may come down from the hills to steal the family's laundry while they are at the movies. He remembers that the snipers are still capable of inflicting harm even if the tide of victory has turned to the American side. Shepard conveys these images in a characteristically hyperbolic humorous fashion, but the sense of anxiety must have been agonizing for a child.

Shepard's childhood was thus one of some deprivation and, also, of some excitement. His father was a pilot and a handsome man to boot. Rogers, Sr., who was wounded during World War II—a piece of shrapnel became a permanent fixture in his neck—stayed in the air force after the war ended. His roots had been severed in Illinois when the farm on which he grew up, which had been in the family for six generations, was sold to cover debts. Rogers had married another Midwesterner, who came from a genteel, professional family, Jane Elaine Schook; her forebears are alluded to in

A Lie of the Mind by the father, who mocks them as a family of professionals and "pharmacists." The new bride followed her husband from base to base during the war and after, and also began a teaching career.

In 1955 Rogers, Sr., left the service, feeling a need to establish a rooted future for his family. From this point on, Rogers veered between a strict self-discipline and a self-indulgence that led him further and further into alcoholic binges and fantasy. He worked at various jobs and moved his family first to Pasadena and later to Duarte, a suburban area near Los Angeles but far enough away to retain an agricultural ambience. Rogers, Sr., may have been trying to instill in his children—there were now three of them, two sisters in addition to Sam—the sense of belonging he once felt in Illinois before the family land was sold. The move to California occurred in 1955 when Shepard was eleven years old; the new "home" was an avocado ranch with cows and horses to tend as well. Shepard, whose education had been scattered through army bases and then in South Pasadena, spent all his teenage years in Duarte and enjoyed an uninterrupted high school tenure.

For Shepard as he recalls it in his work, Duarte was, in the 1950s, representative small-town America. He particularly liked the animal husbandry life he led there; as a teenager he thought of becoming a professional veterinarian. Shepard also loved working beside and for his father. The elder Rogers was demanding on the boy but also demanding on himself when he was not suffering from alcoholic bouts. Rogers, Sr., had returned to high school to finish an education interrupted by his World War II service and to earn a degree in education in order to become a teacher. A talented drummer, he also played in a band to earn extra income. It seems apparent that Shepard's father provided a role model for the boy. Yet, while Shepard admired his father and took pride in living up to his father's demands, he felt an antagonism to the man whose shifting moods and lack of family responsibility were so unpredictable. Quarrels arose between father and son; that noisy and dangerous aura of rebellion of youth against age, of violence against authority, surfaced in Shepard's teenage years, but at the same time it was tempered with a correspondingly strong love for small-town American values. Shepard joined the 4-H Club in high school (an organization he would satirize in *Curse of the Starving Class,* his most recognizable treatment of life in Duarte); he worked during the summers as a stable hand and as an orange picker; he tended sheep on his father's ranch, and he even won a prize for one at the State Fair. He also was a typical teenager of the fifties (though at the head of the class) in his passion for the movies and movie culture. His heroes were cowboys and mythic Western heroes, his icons were rugged movie stars who conveyed paternal, fisted strength and the wisdom of Solomon with no second thoughts. Burt Lancaster was one of those idols, as was Spencer Tracy. In his book of memoir prose-poems, *Motel Chronicles,* Shepard writes in an entry (dated April 28, 1981, but serving as a remembrance of things past) how he kept "praying for a double bill of *Bad Day at Black Rock* and *Vera Cruz.*"

If Shepard was a typical California teenager in his movie heroes and in his love for animals and in his obsession with the opposite sex, he also deviated into nonconformist behavior. Vivian M. Patraka and Mark Siegel report in their study, *Sam Shepard,* that Shepard took Benzedrine just before he broke the high-school league's 220 track record; that he, like James Dean, blew off tension by drag racing; and that he once stole, with a friend, a sports car in order that the two of them could drive the car into Mexico for the fun of it. Patraka and Siegel report that Shepard was arrested in Big Bear, California, for making an obscene gesture at the sheriff's wife. Such instances of outlawry may well be as typical of teenagers as their disobedience to parentally approved guidelines, and their incidence suggests that Shepard's rebellious and anarchic streak made itself known during his high-school days. It may be Shepard's pattern to exhibit a perfect record in order to break it with an outlandish act; it may be a form of self-punishment—the branding of the Cain "stigma" as a reflection of his broken home.

Shepard's nonconformist streak also displayed itself in his friendship with one of the few blacks in Duarte and in his high school, Charles Mingus, Jr., the son of the famous jazz musician. Father was working in New York, but the son Charlie was growing up in Duarte along with Shepard. Shepard and Mingus were to have a quarrel during their high-school days (neither apparently has remembered the cause of it) that estranged them until Shepard came to call on Mingus in a diner on the black side of town and later defended him in a brawl. Shepard's friendship with Mingus and his growing awareness of his differences with California and American conventions did not at this point alienate him from his environment: he still planned to become a small-farm owner and rancher and/or veterinarian when he enrolled in 1969 in Mount San Antonio Junior College to study agricultural science.

Shepard joined a church acting company, the Bishop's Company Repertory Players, after graduation from high school and while he was a student at college; the work rescued him from a hysterical family situation and provided opportunity for his dramatic talent. Its avowed purpose was the promotion of Christian values through dramatized productions, but the group was more involved with theater than with religious proselytizing. Its members were young people who loved to act, direct, work on sets and designs, and who loved the camaradarie experience of theater; they were utilizing what was at hand to satisfy their desires and goals, and while their spirits were in the right lane, their choice of plays was eclectic and ecumenical. For one of their performances a black actor was needed, and Shepard thought of Charlie Mingus. Shepard went to a largely segregated black diner to ask Mingus if he would take the part. Mingus recalls that he was impressed with Shepard's walking into foreign turf—he was the only white in the place. Mingus accepted the part, a minor role in Thornton Wilder's *The Skin of Our Teeth,* but during his first performance he exploded at what he saw as white racism in the play. He broke a chair on stage, cursed out the play and white racists, and created a one-man storm of abuse. The largely white and young audience chased after him; Mingus found safety, hidden in the top of a tree, while the angry crowd searched for him. Only Shepard saw where Mingus was (both literally and metaphysically), and speaking sotto voce to his friend up the tree, Shepard told him he admired his courage and his dramatic criticism. The two became friends again, though Mingus left town soon after, when his father summoned him to come to New York. Variant dramatizations of this incident—that is, a rebel's escape from an angry mob—are found in Shepard's work, often disguised in other trappings. In one of the versions a group of underprivileged teens beat up a group of rich white kids in front of a diner. The white kids had provoked the fight when they grew angry at the black and lower-class kids coming into *their* diner. The parameters of feeling are clearly those of rich against poor, black against white, underprivileged against privileged, secure against homeless. What matters in Shepard's version is that the underdog comes out on top by asserting his independence and refusing to remain a victim.

All during this time Shepard's father was experiencing a profound erosion of self-confidence. His father's alcoholism was manifesting itself more blatantly, and he could not hold onto jobs for any sustained period of time; he disappeared for weeks at a stretch, having wandered off to desert holes and hideaways where he lived alone or at bars until he fell asleep. Shepard's mother was apparently a very forgiving woman, and she wished to hold the family together at all possible cost—she often followed her husband to his desert outposts to bring him home and sober him up, and she accepted her husband's sexual desertions. At a certain point she surrendered to despair: she began to hold the family together without a man at the head of the constellation. Though she did not reject the father, she ignored him and lost faith in his protestations of reform whenever he reappeared. (The outlines of the mother's attitude can be seen most pointedly in the portrait of Ella in *Curse of the Starving Class,* but it is also apparent in each of the plays in the family trilogy, and in Shepard's *A Lie of the Mind.*)

Shepard indulged in his own activities to ease away the parental problematics of his life. He began writing during his high-school days—he wrote a play that he remembers as a poor imitation of Tennessee Williams—but there is no evidence that he took the work seriously or harbored a desire for a writing career. In his own words, he wanted to be a rock'n'roll star as early as his high-school days; writing was an amusement but secondary to his passion for rock music and its world of glamorous icons. There is a story that a beatnik in his high school, whom all the "straight" kids shunned, threw Shepard a copy of Samuel Beckett's *Waiting for Godot.* Shepard read it, liked it, and is reported to have said that Beckett's play convinced him *anything* could be done with words, just as music could change anyone's world. Shepard however did not pursue any further reading in Beckett. (Later, in New York, he would do so, and also read Bertolt Brecht, who became the playwright he worshiped. Still, it is probable that Beckett's majestic absurdism had a profound, if unannounced, effect on him.)

Shepard's reading was, in any case, erratic. He consumed all the Beats he could get his hands on, and he knew his Allen Ginsberg, Jack Kerouac, and Gregory Corso. Not surprisingly, he identified with them, but Shepard was, aside from performing in bands, more interested in acting than in writing. As an actor he could be engaged with peers and friends; he could work in a group; as a writer he was a loner. As an actor he could enjoy immediate gratification; as a writer he might never know satisfaction, and certainly not know it till the maturity of self-judgment convinced him of his own worth.

By all accounts Shepard was a talented actor in his school productions. His good looks, his intensity, his willingness to work hard, contributed to success on the school stage. He was also a marvel in his ability to improvise; the talent for stopping a script in its narrative drive and moving into character gear/monologue had its beginning in those days.

Shepard had completed three semesters at Mount San Antonio Junior College in 1963 when the Bishop's Company Repertory Players invited him to join them on a cross-country tour. Aware such a move meant a likely end to his college career, Shepard made the decision to leave. Probably the cover of church orientation and sponsorship allowed him, at nineteen and in a state of divided loyalties and goals, to find the strength to depart. When the company reached New York some months later, Shepard decamped and went off to visit Mingus, who was now living in an apartment on the Lower East Side. Shepard moved in with Mingus, who got him a job as a busboy at The Village Gate. The Village Gate in the 1960s was the premier spot for jazz and improvisational music at the time; many of the counterculture performers made their home there at one time or another. Only once did Shepard lose his cool at his job: one evening, as described in several accounts, he rolled a tray of drinks down a customer's lap purposefully—the man represented for Shepard everything corrupt in American values. Shepard was fired that night, but stayed on in New York, for he had been introduced by Mingus to Ralph Cook, the founder of Theater Genesis in St. Mark's Church on the Bowery; all three were working at the time at The Village Gate. Shepard had shown Cook his first play, and Cook agreed to put it into production. On October 10, 1964, a double bill of Shepard's *Cowboys* and *Rock Garden* was performed at Theater Genesis.

Cowboys may be reconstructed in general outline by a reading of *Cowboys No. 2*, which Shepard says is a rewriting by memory of the lost script. The play derives its vitality from the antics of two urban cowboys who shoot the breeze on New York City streets and who play harmless jokes on people crossing their paths. The "cowboys" are Shepard and Mingus, who literally played cowboy-and-Indian games on Avenue C during the time they roomed together.

The period of the 1960s was an exciting time for young and experimental playwrights. It was the period when off-off-Broadway came into being, and plays, written by nonprofessionals, could be mounted cheaply and enthusiastically. It was the period when the great improvisational theater groups gained the spotlight for their way of theater. It was the period when the Living Theatre achieved its world renown under the direction of Julian Beck and Judith Malina. Jack Gelber's *The Connection,* an early and probably the most influential example of the new-theater consciousness, made its debut in 1959; its influence was to continue for decades on young dramatists, among them Sam Shepard. The Open Theatre, under the direction of Joseph Chaikin, came into being in the early sixties. Working with Chaikin, an actor and writer as well as director, and still active in the theater despite his poor health, were such new and beginning talents as Jean-Claude van Itallie, Megan Terry, Kenneth H. Brown, and Rochelle Owens. Shepard took classes with Chaikin; he still regards Chaikin as the "master," a sage who showed him how to make theory bloom into theatrical reality and maturity. Improvisation is one of the chief tenets in the Open Theatre credo. It manifested through "transformation exercises." Under Chaikin's direction, classes were held in which individual actors were asked to transform themselves into a specified voice, whether one of anger, grief, joy, or any variation of emotional response and "place" of spiritual content. The idea was to make the actor more "open" in his interpretations. By opening himself to emotion as brought into being by the demands of a situation given without warning or time for preparation, the actor could come into contact with his deepest reality of parallel to the playwright's script. The transformation would be in the context of the script; it would be a discovery, not a revision of the playwright's words. The process of transformation thus becomes a collaborative exercise, one in which all players, including writer and director as well as actor, are subject to a premise and its reigning emotion. The emotional reign creates the magic that unleashes greater awareness of expression of what is locked up in the content's soul. Even at this present date, Shepard utilizes the spirit of transformational exercises. Like his concept of "play," transformation becomes a liberation of monologue. In the 1960s the practice was particularly important to the young playwright, because it gave intellectual support to a revolutionary mood in the theater. Shepard and other young playwrights could become rebels within their cause of craft.

Transformation as a methodology is similar to the system exemplified by Konstantin Stanislavsky and incorporated into the

Method style of acting in the 1950s by such teachers, directors, and producers as Elia Kazan, Lee Strasberg, Stella Adler, and Cheryl Crawford. What distinguishes it from prior movements is that at a certain point, and suddenly, the actor is asked to transform himself into another character in the mise-en-scène, to become another actor in the "placed" drama. The sudden transformation, to which the actor brings his immediate past associations, is likely (in Open Theatre view) to bring new revelation because no time is allowed for guarded reactions or for planned defense/attacks of rationalized characterization. In the height of the intuitive moments of transformation, the actor has only his own sympathetic associations upon which to rely.

Other groups also influenced Shepard. The best known are Ellen Stewart's La Mama Theatre Company, still in existence today, and a force that changed theater history. Joe Cino's Cafe Cino laid the groundwork for off-off-Broadway achievements by providing an inexpensive dinner (or lunch) theater. In Cafe Cino many of the first plays of playwrights who would later achieve prominence were mounted while cappuccino was being served to enthusiastic and sometimes bewildered audiences. Cafe Cino became the 1960s version of samizdat, but for economic and gustatory rather than political reasons.

Antonin Artaud and his theory of ritual as an ordering of reality was another vital force on the scene. Beckett, and his dramatic enactments of silence and absurdism, was still another dominant force. Barbara Garson's *MacBird,* an outrageous and deeply impassioned protest against corruption in high places, typified one corner of the decade's public stage. In the play, which is patterned on *Macbeth,* President John Kennedy is murdered by order of a figure resembling Lyndon Johnson, who wishes to succeed to the throne of American politics.

Although Shepard's politics—indeed his natural bias against political demonstrations and gamesmanship—differs from Garson's, the two represent the spirit of an age in which the contours of drama were stretched wider to allow wild imagination as a form of reality. Both were in the right place at the right time for their careers to take shape. The same may be said for other playwrights of this period, all of them using liberties with history, some of them confrontationally political. Among these dramatists, several of whom were in workshops with Shepard, are John Guare, Maria Irene Fornes, Lanford Wilson, Terrence

McNally, Arthur Kopit, Paul Foster, Rochelle Owens, Megan Terry, Adrienne Kennedy, Rosalyn Drexler, Kenneth Bernard, and Kenneth Brown.

Yet, if Shepard's success is in part due to the good fortune of being in New York in the 1960s, his achievements have other, and timeless causes. Unwilling to pander to political temporality—he is a man of conservative political tastes or at most, moderate liberalism—Shepard has been a loner in the predominantly liberal-political theater world. His isolation however is no greater, and no more damaging to his work, than was his awareness of difference from his Duarte colleagues.

Most of the reviews of Shepard's first produced plays, *Cowboys* and *Rock Garden,* were negative; Shepard explicitly scored Jerry Tallmer of the *New York Post* for not understanding the off-off-Broadway movement and for writing about it abundantly. Shepard was however very fortunate in having the *Village Voice* reviewer Michael Smith, write about his work. On the basis of Smith's review, attention was paid to Shepard's future.

Rock Garden, set in three scenes, is, in Shepard's words, the story of his leaving his mother and father. What Shepard means by his statement is that the play provides the milieu of a home in which no attention is paid to the cries of its young child. In the first scene the techniques of audience alienation, as Shepard understood it from his favorite playwright, Bertolt Brecht, is at work. Three people—father, daughter, son—are at the kitchen table. No word is spoken between them. The boy and girl are drinking milk. The father is reading a magazine. The girl spills her milk. Blackout. The second scene opens in the bedroom of the mother of the house. Long-suffering, she now whines about her life to her son. She asks him—he is dressed only in his underwear—to bring her blankets to keep her warm; she asks him to perform several errands. Each time he leaves and returns he has put on a new item of clothing. By the end of the scene he is fully clothed. The mother first speaks of a snack she remembers fondly—angels on horseback—it is a combination of salt crackers and marshmallows toasted over an open fire. The mother says the boy's father loves angels on horseback; she says he would spend whole nights over the fire toasting them. Although she says the father never leaves the house anymore, his face used to get ruddy from the fire over which he cooked his angels on horseback. The various references to food signify the father's indulgence as an evasion of emotional response. The mother will also complain that, though they live near the beach, the father rarely goes into the open air. The mother will tell how the father has become a recluse living up in the attic with his cats: he will eat only when he is alone. Though he is perfectly healthy, he refuses all household tasks: the windows need putty, for example, but the father generally finds an excuse not to do the job. The mother in despair has taken to bed, the father to his privacy. As the mother concludes her litany of complaints, the father appears in the room. Like the son, he is fully dressed and looks perfectly normal.

In scene 3 both the father and the son are found in their underwear. They are the only two on stage; their equalization of dress suggests that Shepard is criticizing the father for what the boy has yet to learn and make a choice upon. The two do not talk to each other. They listen, or pretend to listen, while each in turn engages in a long monologue about what *he* wants from life. The father tells of his one passion: he wants to build a rock garden. All his energy is pent up in the dream-construction of a rock garden that will be his desert island, his refuge from the world of people surrounding his daily rounds. The boy is patient at first, then dives aggressively into his monologue. He talks about his primary concern: his initiation into, his enjoyment of, his obsession with, sex. He tells of his various triumphs, his fantasies of how to improve on his formidable achievements, his desires for a world in which masturbation takes care of everything. His words fall over each other in a flood; as he ends his monologue he has come all over himself.

By equating the father and son through their dual appearance in their underwear, and in placing each of their monologues in sequential context, Shepard is suggesting a pattern of similarity between the two males. Both the boy and the father live in a masturbatory haze; each is king of his fantasyland, but king only so long as he does not leave his land. Shepard seems to be suggesting that the boy has a chance to break free of the stifling house in which he is a prisoner of his own fantasies and those of his mother and father. For the boy does masturbate even if he does not communicate; he does something, while the father only talks about building his rock garden. The father's life has ended in a retreat to his attic, and one might argue he needs no rock garden enclosure: the rock garden is simply a more majestic rationalization of his essential condition. The father is irredeemably enclosed; the boy lies in a womb of self-centeredness, but he can move.

For a play written when he was not yet twenty-one, and for what is only his second produced effort, *Rock Garden* is a surprisingly finished work. Its linear design, its abstract air, its mythic dialogue, are among Shepard's most accessible works. It also points to some of his more ambitious later achievements.

3

The Plays: 1965–1967

In 1965 an event occurred in Shepard's life about which little has been written; some critics probably feel the less said about it the better. Yet the consequences of the event may be more pervasive in Shepard's writing than have been acknowledged. It is clear that sometime during 1965 Shepard was called up for examination by the US Selective Service. He failed the examination by claiming heroin addiction. Although Shepard has not denied this fact, reports of which have been published in earlier biographical and critical studies, two questions remain at issue. The first is, was Shepard's heroin addiction a "supposed"[1] addiction as reported in earlier critical studies? It is known that Shepard had used drugs on occasion and at times was reported into "heavy drugs." Yet Shepard exhibits none of the qualities of a heavy drug user, or user of heavy drugs, unless his temper outbursts may be considered as such. Temper flare-ups, and reports of violent behavior, are what Shepard associates with characters bearing his autobiographical data. Such temper tantrums then are Shepard's guilt by association with his evaluation of himself, but, even granting that Shepard may be an occasionally violent man, as he seems to wish to suggest in his fictional persona (a description that his friends and associates disown), his connection to heroin is marginal. The point is, Shepard did not lie in that he revealed he took drugs, but did he promote the truth in saying so? The moral issue is twin-headed: is a literal truth an evasion of the real truth? Is answering a question without giving any explanation a moral lapse, when indeed one has probably not been asked to explain, since draft boards are notorious for their impatience with interviewees who give explanations? Is Shepard's action then a matter of truth or a lapse of it? If he was not an addict, but someone who indulged in drugs sporadically and thus is exonerated from that charge, does he bear any responsibility for not indicating his marginality to the dependence? This second question is more troubling than the first, for it raises a moral issue by evasion of a moral issue. If Shepard wished to avoid the draft because of his anti-Vietnam War sentiments, such a declaration would be recognized as a moral stance. If he wished to avoid selective service as a conscientious objector, such a declaration would be accepted as a right of principle. To avoid the draft for other reasons, whatever they be, becomes a different issue, and consequently a debatable one. On this issue Shepard has remained adamantly silent. Of course he has a right to do so. But his silence does not make the puzzling history go away. A case in point: Peter Stampfel, the lead musician in the Holy Modal Rounders, knew Shepard well in the 1960s. They played in a musical group for several years and traveled across country on several tours. Stampfel has said, "I've read things about how he was a wild drug-taker during the Sixties, but he never was. I never saw him even smoke marijuana—he didn't like it. He always disliked the whole hippie-type image. When we played a couple of colleges, a lot of the girls thought he was a greaser because he had short hair and he wore a leather jacket. He obviously was not a hip person. He was looked on like a low-class hitter type—that's the way a lot of girls pegged him in 1969" (quoted in Oumano, 73).

Shepard himself is quoted by Ellen Oumano: "To me the influence of the sixties and the off-off-Broadway theatre and the Lower East Side was a combination of hallucinogenic drugs, the effects of those drugs on the perceptions of those I came in contact with, the effects of those drugs on my own perceptions, the Vietnam War, and all the rest of it which is now all gone" (95). Oumano comments that "despite his incredible luck to be in New York during the emergence of the off-off Broadway, Shepard came to think of the Sixties as awful and dismissed the importance of the entire off-off-Broadway movement" (95).

Yet it is also a fact that Shepard, in 1971, before departing for self-exile in England, claimed he needed to get away from the drug scene and from the world into which he had sunk. While in England, Shepard was arrested on a minor drug charge. And it is also true, in literary terms, that many Shepard plays are "trips" of one kind or another, quests in which the characters are high on drug trips and/or emotional/chemical waves involving ecstasy, paranoia, and a universe of overwhelming music.

In an article printed in *American Film: Magazine of Film and Television Arts* (October 1984), Shepard is credited with a history of drinking and drug problems. Presumably Shepard gave such information to the writer of the article, Blanche McCrary Boyd, since the rest of the piece is based on information given in an interview by Shepard a few months earlier in the Staab House restaurant in Santa Fe, New Mexico. Boyd writes: "Inheritance has its complications, and Sam developed drinking—and drug—problems of his own. In the Sixties he became dependent on crystal methedrine, and in 1971 moved to England to clean up. But when he kicked the drugs, he replaced one addiction with another." Shepard became a heavy tequila drinker, and only since his relationship with Jessica Lange began in 1981, has the "desire to drink excessively left him."

Such is Shepard's own view of his drinking and drug problems as filtered through memory and self-knowledge. Having raised these questions, it is not necessary to dwell on them. A man is many men, as Shepard has shown in his work. A man is a different man on different occasions, as Shepard knows from his transformational exercises. Shepard is a devoted father, a caring family man, a friend to those he considers in need and whose needs he wishes to consider. And his greatness as a writer is not affected by what has already passed in his life, since the works signifying his achievement have been written. Shepard's literary achievement is secure. I raise the questions here not because of any wish to besmirch Shepard's character, but because I think Shepard must have had a profound reaction to what he did, and only when one knows Shepard's attitude to this issue, then and now, will one be able to know how he has reacted to what he committed that day in 1965. The act he took, whether motivated by factual truth, by political/moral testament, or by any other concern, has already affected his work; it may do so again, as all profound issues reverberate throughout a person's life. It cannot deny Shepard's achievements as a writer.

Consider what is really at issue here: Shepard, in his statement to the draft board, would again be coming into conflict with his father, whose one shining accomplishment was his army air force record. In the eyes of Shepard's father, the son's actions must have constituted an enormous treachery personally, familially, and patriotically. Yet Shepard's father presumably knew the powers of temptation to addiction and so could forgive a fellow addict. Shepard has written a great deal about his conflicts with his father, and about their similarities, in disguised facts easily dissembled, the clues to which dissembling are given by the author himself gladly. Shepard has even written a wonderfully comic play in which he exposes his own method of disguise and dissembling, *Suicide in B♭.*

Yet he has not approached this subject-material except once; he has apparently buried it in a garden of the past.

Up to Thursday, one of Shepard's plays written soon after his draft-board experience, is, at least according to one critic, intimately connected with that experience. In a review in *Newsday* (February 11, 1965) Murry Fryman wrote, "Shepard, 21, has said that the play was written as a reaction to his being drafted into the Army. Well, the draft affects all of us differently." The play is Shepard's only presentation of material remotely connected with that experience. It has not been published, mainly because, like several other plays Shepard wrote in quick succession in 1965, it is a poor work. Shepard has disowned it, as well as *Dog* and *Rocking Chair,* produced together on a double bill at La Mama ETC on February 10, 1965.

Up to Thursday has eight characters—Young Man, First Man, Second Man, Third Man, Terry, Sherry, Larry, and Harry. In its singsong and allegorical names, the play is part of the technique Shepard uses in other, later work. Set in two scenes, it tells no narrative story, though there is some action. In the first scene a crane lifts a rock up from the ground as workmen pin a young man down on the ground. In the background is played a Beatles recording of their song, "I Saw Her Standing There." The scene ends with applause from behind the curtain as the rock is lifted up and the young man is pinioned down. In the second scene the young man is lying in bed clothed only in his underwear. An American flag covers his body. A game of knocking people off chairs ensues—Terry, Sherry, Larry, and Harry take turns sitting and knocking others down. The Young Man runs across the stage in his underwear, inquiring if a woman has come back with his clean underwear, insisting she promised to do so. Back in bed, he pulls the American flag over his body, but he keeps harping on the expected woman with clean underwear. A conversation between Larry, Harry, Sherry, and Terry begins about the merits of running, and whether such activity is good for the human back. The construction men return on stage and lead off the Young Man as if he is their prisoner. Shepard writes in his direction that the Young Man "looks back and forth at the two men as they slowly walk up to him and grab each of his arms." Again the Beatles record, "I Saw Her Standing There," is played. The Young Man is removed from the stage by the construction men. Whether he is being abducted, arrested, and/or *drafted* is left to be decided in the image Shepard presents of the scene. Whatever his plight, some hanky-panky is going on under the American flag as Sherry and Harry have climbed into the Young Man's bed and are fooling around under the flag.

The elements in Shepard's play will become familiar: the nameless Young Man, the representation of social types through mocking mimicry, the musical backgrounds as commentary, and the blackout on stage as a curtain indicator. The references to underwear and to laundry will become familiar imagery as well. Although it is difficult to assign one coherent meaning to the actions in the play, the suggestion of the Young Man's abduction, imprisonment, rape of spirit, and the construction men's glee in seizing him, seems apparent. Shepard is presenting the plight of the dissident in an indifferently hostile society through the image of the young loner stripped to his underwear and facing a construct of homogenized opinion. The applause as the construction workers suggestively brutalize his options of staying in bed/getting out of bed does seem a comment on social attitudes. Most critics however did not find much meaning in the play, though several applauded its humor, stagecraft, and dialogue. Michael Smith, in the *Village Voice* (February 13, 1965) was again Shepard's most astute critic. He wrote that the play "uses ordinary actors for abstract ends in a play that has no naturalistic level at all." Smith judged the play "funny on a sharp, immediate, original level" but wrote it was "entirely lacking in content" and that while it was "extraordinarily inventive," it was "no more than an adroit diversion." Smith went on to compare *Up to Thursday* with Shepard's two other plays of that month. "Two of his new plays were given last weekend at the Cafe La Mama. *Dog*, although similarly low in content, was even more economical, tight in structure, and wholly effective. *The Rocking Chair* attempted to talk about some of its characters' actual concerns but bogged down in apparently untransformed emotions."

Up to Thursday was first produced by Theatre 1965 (via its Playwrights Unit) on November 23, 1964, at the Village South Theatre as a result of Shepard's barging into Edward Albee's apartment in Greenwich Village with a suitcase of manuscripts. The famous playwright responded to the younger playwright's audacity with amusement and interest. Albee selected *Up to Thursday* from the mass of manuscripts in the suitcase and brought it to the attention of his partners in Theatre 1965, Richard Barr and Clinton Wilder. It was as a result of the revival of the play, mounted in February 1965 at the Cherry Lane Theatre, that Shepard met the young actress Joyce Aaron, who was auditioning for the part of

Sherry. The part demanded a series of monologues in which the only signifiers were laughing words. Aaron's laughter, and what she did with it, intrigued Shepard, and thus began their two-year intimate relationship. The two became lovers. Shepard moved into Aaron's apartment, and Aaron introduced Shepard to influential people in the theater, among them Joseph Chaikin, Richard Gilman, and Jean-Claude van Itallie of the Open Theatre; to the director Jacques Levy; and to Wynn Handman, the founder of American Place Theatre.

Herself a writer (*Acrobatics*) as well as an actress with one Obie to her credit, Aaron still lives in the Greenwich Village neighborhood she and Shepard shared in their youth. She remembers him as a "natural poet," a writer who did not read other authors but who wrote out of the images in his mind. Aaron does not think of Shepard as a heroin addict and says "he never took drugs to write." She says he was an extraordinarily prolific writer in his first years in New York, and tells the story of a ruined suitcase that contained many of his scripts. She had put some of her things along with Shepard's manuscripts in a suitcase that she boarded in the basement of her cousin's (Hope Wurmfeld's) house. When the basement was flooded, everything in it was carted away. Shepard did not know which, nor how many, plays were lost; they were his only copies. Shepard's productivity is also confirmed by Richard Gilman, the well-known drama critic, who met Shepard for the first time at an Open Theatre session (Aaron, an old friend of Gilman, introduced them). At their first meeting, Shepard, twenty-one years old and "looking like a 12-year-old blond Midwestern skinny kid" (in Gilman's words), announced he had written hundreds of plays.

Hope Wurmfeld remembers Shepard as a "nice, decent person who loved to kid and play around." A professional photographer (her photograph of Shepard was the first one of him to appear on a dust jacket), Wurmfeld said it was hard to get Shepard to play at being serious for his photo sittings: he often, as he did at her photo session, jumped in and out of ashcans while she was "shooting" him. For Wurmfeld, Shepard was cute but not good-looking—he was "skinny and gangling. He didn't get handsome till he grew older." According to Wurmfeld, Shepard would park Joyce Aaron's car in New York anywhere he found a convenient parking space; he was used to his Duarte ways where parking was no problem. The result was an avalanche of parking tickets, which Shepard ignored. One day Aaron and her friends pooled their money, put the cash in a bag with the traffic tickets, and Aaron went off to traffic court. She was cutely full of an innocent guile, and the judge listened sympathetically: he scaled down the fines.

Aaron's courtroom escapade is another way she took care of Shepard's needs and saved him from distractions. She liked doing that, Wurmfeld remembers.

Many of Shepard's plays of the sixties are based on his experiences with Aaron, though truthful to biographic fact only in essence. *Chicago,* Shepard's sixth-produced play, is one of these works deriving from his association with Aaron. Shortly after their relationship began, Aaron got a job with a theater production in Chicago; she did not wish to leave Shepard, but she also did not wish to forsake an important career opportunity. Out of this experience came the transformed script of *Chicago.* (One ironic consequence of the experience for Aaron is that she refused an offer to work with Gerome Ragni and Jim Rado in order that she would have time for Shepard when he visited her in Chicago. The Ragni-Rado project turned out to be *Hair.*)

Chicago opens with the protagonist Stu sitting in a bathtub. His girlfriend Joy is baking biscuits. When Stu makes light of her biscuits, she throws some at him. He eats one while sitting in the tub. Joy climbs into the tub with him, then gets out after a few verbal strokes of affection. Stu begins to impersonate an old lady criticizing the morals and values of young people; he clearly is getting back at Joy for her desertion of him from the tub. Then Stu goes into a monologue of what it's like to be a fish when fishermen come after you with their hooks. While Stu is lamenting the plight of fishing victims, several people are phoning Joy to ask her if she's taken "the job." They congratulate her when she says yes, and they wish her well; they promise to come to see her off when she leaves for Chicago. Stu objects to her leaving, but he does not get out of the tub to do anything about the situation. The tub is his safe pond, still off-limits to any voracious fishermen. Joy goes offstage with a cart full of luggage as several of her friends appear on different parts of the stage to wave good-bye kisses. Alone in the tub, Stu talks about the tide going out at night, and about the possibility of his getting stuck on the beach one night: the wind will be cold and crack his skin; he'll bleed from the exhaustion of running up the beach to get out of the cold wind; he'll experience cramps and muscle rigidity. Anxiety will grip him, but he'll make it up the beach.

At this point in his manic monologue, Stu jumps out of the tub and begins his lecture on proper breathing methods. He tells the audience how to inhale and exhale, how to get in stride with the rhythms of living. The lecture becomes Stu's rationale for the kind of life he has chosen to lead; his breathing exercises are his terms and conditions of living. Standing dry and clothed after having spent a day in his tub, Stu is an ambivalent image. For one viewer he may be the frightened schizoid unable to leave his tub for a world with wider opportunities and greater dangers; he may be a rationalizer of his own limitations much like the old lady he was mocking minutes earlier, the kind of old lady who dislikes youth and its sexy, bright promises. From another biographic perspective, the old lady Stu is mocking/mimicking may be a reflection of Shepard's mother cautioning him against promiscuity; she may also be Shepard's imaged fear of his father proclaiming Shepard a lazy parasite. By metaphysical extension, Stu may also represent American culture, or rather that stage of it sinking into entropy. Unable to recreate vitality, unable to function as a vital, ongoing organism, its manifestation in Stu sinks back into decadence, into a sheltering anachronism devoid of emotional currency. (It is interesting to remember what Shepard himself said about the origins of *Chicago:* it started from an image of two people, Mingus and himself, carrying a bathtub through the streets of the lower East Village; Shepard said people did things like that "in those days." *Chicago* becomes his transformation of the image into a reflection of what kind of people carry what kinds of things on their passage through the streets of their living.) Yet another viewer may see in Stu a man in tune with his own rhythm, one who does not need to seek glamour in his life, one who doesn't need the satisfaction of material rewards that employment brings. Though Stu has let Joy go, and has remained in his tub without much protestation, the question remains: is he a fool or a wise man? Should he have tried to hold onto her? Is he better off without her? Shepard offers little aid to the answer others are guessing. His final image is of Stu encouraging a group of eager students to plunge into a swimming lesson. Stu says to them, "Ladies and Gentlemen, it's fantastic." As the play ends, the audience is no closer to a resolution of the tantalizing questions of Stu's character—con man, self-deceiver, lazy fool, or frightened, pale and wan lover—than he was at the beginning of the very funny goings-on in a tub's tale. He does have the apartment all to himself. But is an apartment, if it means the loss of the girl one loves, worth it? (Shepard was not Stu at this point, since Aaron had him go back to Charlie Mingus's apartment while she was in Chicago. Only after her return to New York did he become "entrenched"— in her words—in her place.)

Originally produced at Theater Genesis in St. Mark's Church on the Bowery on April 16, 1965, under the direction of Ralph Cook, *Chicago* became Shepard's first popular play. (It was revived at Cafe La Mama in March 1966 and given an extended run at the Martinique Theatre in April 1966.) Much of the criticism was favorable; even those who caviled expressed their pleasure at its clever humor. The cavilers objected to Shepard's irresolute ending; they became the first of Shepard's detractors who wanted resolute endings. Shepard, in turn, expressed his disdain for endings; he ranted against the constraints of dramatic resolution that forced a curtain on a drama in progress.

If *Chicago* is a tease, with the playwright unwilling to go all the way to a closure of resolution, it is transparent in its evocation of anxiety. Stu has apocalyptic visions; the world in which he lives is so frightening that he finds getting through it an anxious choice between the dead hooked fish in the sea and the dead living tissue in a sterile world. Even Joy, who ventures out with a cart of luggage, keeps returning on stage with the same cart; she seems to be going nowhere, though she says she is going somewhere. As Stu finishes his breathing lesson on how to hold onto dear life, Joy comes back onstage with her cart. In exactly the same way minutes earlier she had left and returned, she exits like a refugee wandering on a circular path to bring her back to the starting point of nowhere.

Earlier in the year Shepard had two one-act plays produced at La Mama ETC (in February 1965) on a double bill. In an interview originally published in *Theatre Quarterly* in 1974, Shepard is quoted as saying: "I don't remember *Rocking Chair,* except that it was about somebody in a rocking chair." In the high speed in which Shepard was writing at the time, Shepard's memory—or more accurately his lack of memory—of the fate of *The Rocking Chair* does not seem surprising. More perplexing is the account of *Dog,* which Shepard in the *Theatre Quarterly* interview describes as "about a black guy on a park bench, a sort of *Zoo Story*–type play." Shepard's tribute to Edward Albee, by way of imitation, was probably influenced by the fact that Albee had produced him (*Up to Thursday*) as well as by the awareness that *Zoo Story* was one of the seminal off-Broadway plays of the decade. Albee, in addition, had become a champion of Shepard's talents; he would later praise Shepard's *Icarus's Mother* in the *Village Voice*.

Dog is Shepard's first dramatic treatment of a black character, and it proved an unsettling experience. Shepard said in 1974 that "writing about a black guy" [in 1965] was "uncool for a white to write about in America." Given Shepard's involvement with Charles Mingus, the rejection and low-key hostility by black critics to the play must have caused him some consternation. Years later he would experience more anguish over a new drawing of black characters. As a result of his portrait of three black revolutionaries in *Operation Sidewinder,* a controversy ensued that resulted in cancellation of production of the play by Yale University's Drama Department. Michael Feingold, literary manager of the drama department, was the first to discuss the issue with Shepard and to convey the black student protest against what they considered an unfitting portrait. Robert Brustein, head of Yale's Drama School, wanted the production to continue as scheduled, but Shepard withdrew the play. He did not wish to continue the contentious situation; he preferred withdrawal.

Shepard was writing continually in 1965 and 1966; the scripts flowed from his pen, and he had no sense of writer's block or inhibitions. He did not revise during this period, for he believed that revision in some way wounded the spontaneity of the original creative outpouring. Shepard used his interpretation of Jackson Pollock (one of his favorite painters) and "action painting" to justify his way of writing in those days: the splashes of color that came from his pen fell on the paper in a magically predetermined way. Later he would revise his work extensively; he would utilize craft and form before letting his work go public, but in this period of inspired energy he just kept writing. The works that come out of this period do not pay attention to conventional narrative demands; they are Shepard's way of seeing things, and they express his unique vision. Nevertheless they are graspable, and, taken together, they provide a series of recognizable Shepardian conventions. If Shepard's plays lacked a consistent narrative in those days, they had other unifying threads.

It was at about this time that Shepard changed his name from "Steve" Rogers to Sam Shepard. Shepard has said his full name was too long for theater and marquee purposes, "so I dropped the Rogers part of it. The name [Samuel Shepard Rogers] had been in the family for seven generations and my grandmother wasn't too happy about it" (Oumano, 22). Shepard's name change occasioned greater grief for his father, who saw it as a betrayal of faith by his son in his heritage. Shepard would later deal with this conflict and grievance in *The Holy Ghostly;* it was to be one more quarrel between father and son, one further wedge in an allegiance that, no matter how strong its cracks, never totally crumbled.

Charlie Mingus says that Shepard changed his name because he enjoyed the notoriety it caused as a result of mistaken identity with the medical doctor of the same name who was on the front pages of newspapers across the country. The medical Sam Shepard was a young, handsome, well-to-do osteopath in a Cleveland suburb who was convicted of murdering his wife and who spent ten years in prison before being released on appeal. Mingus's version of the name change suggests Shepard had an eye and ear for self-promotion. In addition, Shepard may have felt impelled by a subconscious drive to identify himself as an outsider, as he had done in high school.

Icarus's Mother, produced first at Cafe Cino in New York's Greenwich Village on November 16, 1965, is one of Shepard's one-act plays that has occasioned much commentary as to its "meaning." Everyone seems to know what it is about, but what really is it about? Shepard has said that the idea for the play originated from his epiphany at a Fourth of July celebration in a Milwaukee park (conceivably he was visiting the area with Joyce Aaron). The noise and violence of the fireworks display threw him into a dark illumination about American history, and he felt again a strain of paranoia he considered typical of his country. Shepard put the transcendent thought together with the premise of people revealing themselves in their "play" at a picnic.

Michael Smith, who directed *Icarus's Mother,* wrote in a published foreword that Shepard's plays transcend naturalism and psychological analysis. At the same time, Smith wrote, the plays use naturalism and psychology as their starting point. Ostensibly the play is about the goings-on at a picnic. Bill, Jill, Pat, Howard, and Frank are finishing up their repast on the beach before the scheduled fireworks begin. They are annoyed by the presence of an airplane above them. The plane, they contend, is defiling the natural peace of their day by its skywriting consumerism. Shepard's satire is double-edged, for Jill, Bill, Pat, Frank, and Howard are foolish and pretentious in their animus against the commercialization of the American country scene. There is, for example, nothing to suggest that each of them does not live in a comfortable cocoon spawned by his or her solipsistic social relations. Shepard's technique of using only first names is as well a satirization of the manners of friendship by such types of supposedly sophisticated professionals, while their similarity of taste makes them appear clones of a class. Where they differ is in detail of neurosis, particularly the character Howard, who can become brutish when provoked by others or by figments of his imagination. The action of the play is ignited when one of the other characters, Pat, wants to take a walk on the beach by herself. The others object to her solo turn, reacting as if she is deserting them. It is possible that Pat has "to pee" and that her desire to get away from the affable but tyrannous majority is simply a desire to do her duty without an embarrassing rhetoric of admission. In the squabble that ensues when Pat makes her wants known, Frank, Jill, and Pat *all* walk off to do their duty. Frank returns alone and is told by Howard and Bill that Jill and Pat have a secret for him. Frank says he knows what it is, and he can tell it to Howard and Bill. Howard and Bill tell him to confirm the secret first with Jill and Pat, that is, to make sure he does not disappoint the two women by revealing *their* secret ahead of time. Jill and Pat return shortly afterward and tell a story of a pilot who flew his airplane into a series of wonderful turns in the sky. They were squatting to pee on the beach when his plane approached, and he went wild, flying higher and higher into the sun. Telling the story, Jill declares that Pat threw kisses at the pilot; she encouraged his antics, and his antics in turn drove the two women "nuts." They took off their clothes and ran into the sea to wave him off. At this point, inspired by the two girls' applause, the pilot climbed forty thousand feet and wrote "E equals MC squared" in the sky.

The writing in the sky is significant, for Shepard is reflecting on human aspiration and disillusionment. The energy gained by the mass is relative to that which is able to separate from the mass as well as that with which it is joined; to be a part of the sky and the water and also of the earth is what transcendence is about. For a moment Pat, and possibly Jill, seize that truth. Yet, immediately after Jill has told her story, Howard informs her that Frank has informed him that the pilot and his plane have crashed. The pilot is dead and fishermen are trying to fish his body out of the water. Frank appears at this point to give his version of the firecracker celebration taking place on the beach: it is a description of an apocalypse illuminated in the blaze of the airplane's descent into the sea.

The symbolism in this play is more apparent than in other Shepard plays, where imagery plays a more dominant role. Generally, Shepard prefers the precise and reverberating image to the intellectualized symbol, for symbolism is less spontaneous than its relative image. The pilot doing his tricks in the sky is undeniably an Icarus figure; the plane, foreboding in its power, represents the technology that can rain bombs from the sky and thus produce a contemporary apocalypse. The picnic—that place and event we, as humans, set up as a release from worldly and domestic problems—is our cocoon, our waying-out station. The "meaning" to be gathered from Shepard's play makes its suggestions through these symbols: the five picnickers preferring their safe neurotic world to the profound apocalypse of the airplane pilot. Each of the five picnickers has a monologue to express his discovery of something that's been around him/her for ages. Shepard's revelation of their solipsism is drawn in their anger at the interruption of the airplane onto their plane of reality (or illusion of reality?). The last lines of the play have Bill yelling at Jill to get away from the picnic area. By urging Bill to come down to look at the spoils of the plane crash, Jill is disturbing Bill's peace of mind. By displaying her excitement over the pilot's magnificent gesture, she is interrupting Bill's conception of picnic as rest and retreat. Like Bill, Jill has not transcended the experience of witnessing the crash. The physical thrill and sensation of having been involved superficially in an apocalypse rather than being a tragic part of it is what excites her. Jill's words are apt for her point of view about the occasion: "You guys are missing out."

Perhaps the one character who does transcend the experience at the picnic is Pat. She exhibits the necessary qualifications: she wanted to walk away from her crowd of superficial, rationalizing friends; she was willing to drop her pants and pee in the blazing sun on the beach; she waved the pilot and the plane on as she danced in baptismal waves of exhilaration; she is down at the crash site, aware of the tragedy that the pilot may have died in his glorious parade of tricks for her pleasure. Granted these possibilities, Pat becomes Icarus's mother (in the Greek myth it is the father that Icarus is trying to please; in Shepard's play it is an Icarus-like pilot who is shouting, "Look, Ma, I'm Dancing.") Pat's grief then is profound, for only the finest die in such a syndrome of events: only the finest can die because only the finest are willing to scale heights gloriously unknown. Pitted with her in the "meaning" of the play is the other plane of symbol: the bomber plane, the reach of science and Einsteinian relativity, that makes possible both apocalypse and the debris of scientific potential.

Shepard's next-produced play, *Red Cross,* was his first off-Broadway production. It premiered at the Judson Poets Theater on January 20, 1966. Jacques Levy, who directed it, cast Joyce Aaron in the lead female role. The stage directions indicate that the motel room in which the two protagonists are staying is to be all white; it is to serve as a contrast for the blood that will come down Jim's forehead at the end of the play and for the image of Carol's blood on the pure white snow after her skiing accident.

As the play opens, Jim and Carol are in their motel room. Carol complains about head pains; she says her head is going to burst one day as she is skiing, and although her injured wracked body will be taken away, a stain of blood will remain on the pure white snow. There will be a "white blanket" with just one little red splotch on it. After her monologue of doom, Carol announces she is going off to do some shopping, and tells Jim she will be back at six.

Alone, Jim starts his push-up exercises. He continues them as the maid comes into the room to make up the beds. Jim tells her about his "crabs." He picks one from his leg and gives it to the maid, to show her he isn't fooling around. She looks at it, returns it to him, says she'll take him to the doctor at six if he wants to wait till then. Jim says he is not sure if he can wait, lots of things can happen before six. Jim also wants a country doctor, because he feels those are the best kind, but the maid says there are no country doctors in this town; she'll take him to a town doctor. Jim at this point moves the beds around so that Carol will have his bed and he will have hers; he'll have her clean white sheets, and she'll have his crabs' egg–lice. When the maid says she wants to make up Carol's bed (which is the bed he has been sleeping in), Jim deters her, saying it is not necessary. Jim's irresponsibility in spreading his crabs to Carol's bed is Shepard's dramatization of Jim's rationale about his life with Carol: she's made her bed by living with Jim, so she must lie in it with the crabs as well. It is Jim's value judgment on himself: for in the next moment he talks the maid into taking an imaginary swimming lesson from him. With the "lesson" comes a race whose winner will be the victor in the flight to the finish line. (It is significant that Jim initiates the lesson and the race immediately after telling the maid that he goes swimming to loosen the crabs from his thighs.) When the maid protests that Jim is going too fast, too far, that she is exhausted, Jim becomes annoyed. He indicates that she hasn't got the right spirit, that she lacks discipline. Jim's monologue is a mock celebration of the discipline of the fighting men who won the war for America in the 1940s, and a mock dressing-down of the flabby, pacifist protesters of the 1960s. Having made his point, Jim stops, and the maid begins her monologue. She turns to the audience and tells them she could drown in the lake while swimming, or practicing her swimming, and no one would notice. In time everyone would forget her. The maid goes into a reverie about the water lilies and dragonflies in her lake. Then, exhausted, she stops her lesson and gets up from the floor where she has been swimming. She leaves the room. Jim yells after her that he can take her to a doctor or drive her home if she's *that* tired.

The sense of hours—not time—is deliberately skewered by Shepard throughout the short play. Both Carol and the maid talk about six o'clock as the time they can be with Jim, but the actual, or literal, time is meaningless. And the maid who makes her last job the making of the beds in Jim's room must have other things to do if she says she won't be free till six: she can't be making the beds at five o'clock if Carol has just left moments before to go shopping. Time becomes a quotient of consciousness, an awareness that time has run out on them. When Carol returns after the maid leaves—presumably at six o'clock—she tells Jim that she began to itch in the grocery store in town and that she ran into the toilet to tear her clothes off and kill the bugs crawling across her body. She tells Jim that they will have to change rooms in this motel, because the bugs come from this room.

All during her declamation, Jim has kept his back to her. When she ends her breast-beating, he turns round. Blood is running down his forehead. The stage turns black as Jim and Carol exchange questions with each other of what went wrong. Carol uses the words, *what happened?*, and Jim answers with the question, *When?* The last words by Jim and by Carol emphasize that the play is about injury and disease of a relationship, and that time—or lack of awareness of the waste of time—is an essential element of the goings-on. The ironic allusions to the Red Cross—through the white walls, the accident on the ski slope, the reference to futile medical aid—strengthen the sense that Shepard is talking of a situation in which little, or nothing, can be done except to let the blood fall, the crabs to run their course.

The crabs, the maid had told Jim, could go on biting him "indefinitely for years." Shepard is ironic again in positioning an adverb of indefiniteness and a noun of definite time next to each other.

The assumption may be made that some hope remains in Shepard's use of this oxymoron that there will be an end to endlessness, that some recouping may be left after the demise of relationships. Or, to use a medical allusion, that some recuperation is possible in the leavings of whatever is left in the void of modern existence.

Shepard's very short play *4-H Club,* presented at the Cherry Lane Theatre in September 1965, was written in the same burst of creative energy as that which gave birth to *Icarus's Mother* and *Red Cross.* He takes three young men rooming together in a tenement apartment and has them express their views on cleanliness, neatness, promptness, dependability, loyalty, considerateness—the list could be extended to the virtues listed in the Boy Scout oath, another group in addition to the 4-H Club Shepard mocks. The young men play games with each other as naturally as they breathe. Although it appears that each has a distinct personality—Joe, for instance, is the neat one constantly sweeping away the debris while John and Bob display their dirty, unwashed clothes like a banner and use the broom as a stickpoint for their games playing—it becomes apparent that individual personality is not what Shepard is after capturing here. He is defining, or representing, various aspects of young men doing their own thing. The men are not sure what they want. On the other hand, they do not bewail their uncertainty as a wound. They go on doing their own thing, sometimes complaining, sometimes hyperventilating, but mostly enjoying themselves until their apocalyptic monologues. John and Bob smash cups, the pieces of which Joe sweeps up. John eats an apple, the eating of which becomes a confrontational discussion of health and social-attitudinal problems. Coffee becomes the next item in the verbal melee, a philosophical container leading to the issue of how to drink coffee when all the cups in one's spheres have been smashed. The conversation veers to social responsibility, and Joe tells the story of a young man who mowed lawns, and by so doing became a respected member of the town. When his ambition grew too big for the birches of his town lawns, he left for the big city and further success there. But, as Joe tells it, he left behind a string of brokenhearted ladies who could not find a new young man with the appropriate lawning attitude to life. The ladies' lawns deteriorated, the town entropied, and decadence moved in everywhere. When Joe's story is concluded, the conversation turns to an admission of a general malaise among the young men, a sense that a plague is going to follow the inevitable invasion of rats in the tenement building. There will be no escape from the ravenous creatures, the men agree. John follows with a story about the mandrill, the fiercest baboon in the world, a creature who can kill with a flick of his wrist. Wolverines run in fear from him, staying close to their pack and closing their eyes to blot out the mandrill's awesome presence. John explains that mandrills instinctively close their eyes when faced with unbearable danger. He ends his monologue with another story about creatures who refuse to face things clearly. This story is about a group of passengers who fly to a resort island to spend their vacation in a lavish hotel suite; the suite is in complete contrast with the apartment in which John, Joe, and Bob live in New York. In their hotel room the passengers block out all thoughts of mandrills, or other dangers, by directing their gaze out their luxury hotel window. What they see is a world free from worry and care and from the thrusts of baboons. In this world of John's telling, all one has to do is to savor the sky, with no limit on the duration of the view.

Shepard's play then is about the void in the center of these young men's lives. They can banter, hit each other in buddy play, but when the traffic of the noise becomes still, they cannot bear to hear the sound of their loneliness. As a means of holding off such an awareness, they smash things and indulge in tricks on each other. Their final resort is the statement of a dream place they put into monologues meant only for the attention of others—for Shepard's characters in this play do not wish to listen to themselves. Indeed, their talk is their defense against hearing what they are saying. The play, in this connection, bears affinity with *Chicago,* with the protagonist Stu in his bathtub refusing to leave his womblike, nonwatered swimming hole. *Chicago* is a more dramatized entity of the condition of fear and ambivalence: Stu in that play became an individualized character, whereas in *4-H Club,* Shepard draws on types and ambience. His portrait becomes one of a failure of culture to produce a viable vision of maturity.

Fourteen Hundred Thousand, first produced in 1966 at the Firehouse Theatre in Minneapolis, Minnesota, and later shown on National Educational Television, was another of Shepard's one-act plays that excited interest in his work and encouraged his standing as a celebrated off-Broadway playwright. It also widened his reputation as a dramatic persona: his good looks, his youth, his productivity as a dramatist, and the vitality in his work all became occasions for commentary in the New York press. *Fourteen Hundred Thousand,* however, had a briefer run than Shepard's usual fleeting mountings, both because of its experimentality and its apparent obscurity and because of production quarrels that led to a less than harmonious staging of the work. Shepard, who was becoming increasingly aware of the direction of his work, quarreled with the director, Sydney Schubert Walter, and exerted pressure to have things done according to his (pre)conceptions. Shepard, for example, wanted a bare stage on which the characters stood out clearly against the only prop on stage, the eponymous bookshelves; the director wanted to utilize more props to create more action on stage. Shepard insisted he was after a contrast between the naturalistic beginning of the play and its contrasting expressionism at the end, while the director wished to emphasize the language in the play as expressionistic coding from its first utterance.

Fourteen Hundred Thousand is indeed about language, but Shepard is asking, To what point? Language, and wisdom in print, is available to those who would take it from the fourteen hundred thousand or so books to be put on the shelves in the apartment Shepard is creating on stage, but the shelves are never going to get built. That is the point of the play. For Shepard is talking about people never getting beyond the printed word, or the wooden shelf, never going into the ecstasy of vision that literature and writing is about. He constantly refers to the puzzle: why build shelves for books that will never be read again, if indeed they were ever read in the first place? A bookshelf, Shepard seems to be saying, is only as good as what has been taken off it and aggrandized for personal meaning. He represents his ideas in a young couple, Donna and Tom. Donna wants a place for her books, a place where her books can be seen, where they can remind her of all the pleasure they once brought her and where others can see how much Donna has read, or at least how many books she has collected. Tom, her husband, on the other hand, believes books should be thrown away in a trash can once they've been read; on a bookshelf they only collect and make noticeable the dust they collect. Donna's conspicuous consumption and Tom's practical considerations of his outer space are now played out against the view that Ed, the handyman and friend of the couple, signifies. Ed is willing to help build the bookshelves, but he says he can't stay long to help because he has to get away to the country. Ed has been given a cabin in the country by friends, and he's promised them to go there this weekend. Tom and Donna have a discussion of whether it was very "nice" of Ed's friends to lure him away when they need him. They also discuss the issue of the cabin gift to Ed: in giving it, did Ed's friends think of it as a donation to Ed, as charity, as a goodwill gesture? The young couple bring Ed to the thorny journey point of discovering who his friends really are—the condescending ones in the country who give away a cabin they do not need, or the young couple in town trying to resurrect literature through the construction of bookshelves and in need of a good handyman like Ed?

The philosophical game of bookshelves—what they mean built and unbuilt, and whether they should be built or deconstructed—is played out further when Mom and Pop come to help the young married couple. Mom and Pop wonder if all the books should be brought up the many flights of stairs—there are, after all, so many of them (steps and books), and Mom and Pop are not so young anymore. Besides, the possibility of a future after all the books are brought up is not entirely bright: it is likely that everyone who came to help build the bookshelves and bring up the books will disperse after the job is done. Mom begins a reverie at this point about the comfort that books bring, particularly when it is snowing outside and one is inside reading. Books take on meaning for her by light of the position in which she reads them (reversing the usual order of reading books in the position of light shed on them by a bulb and/or human commentator). Mom is thus a progenitor of the mother in *A Lie of the Mind,* a mother who yearns for the purity of snow, for a return to the prelapsarian time when she believed in the purity of nature and before the circumstances of time played dirty tricks on her.

The mother's reminiscence about the snows of yesteryear lead Donna to state her dream of a snowy Thanksgiving with the accompaniment of a roaring log fire inside a big, cozy house, and turkey and cranberry on the dining-room table. Facing the table, or somewhere in Donna's picture of the mind, are books, like background music orchestrating a tone of quietly joyous satisfaction with life. Donna's monologue and the others that follow by Tom, Ed, and Pop reveal different aspects of books: books as pets, books as atmosphere, books as duty, books as pleasure, books as a means of holding the family together. Significantly, books as learning is not notated in any of the monologue/reveries. In this incremental scheme, the bookshelf, or shelves, becomes the wooden record of a family life still to be lived through.

Ed, who has said earlier in the play that he must leave to go away to the country, keeps coming back to help out with bringing up the books and with constructing the bookshelves. What he, and the other characters, see, however, is a dismantling of their work as soon as they have nearly completed it: the shelves keep falling down as soon as they are *almost* put up. The explanation is not so difficult: if the bookshelves represent the containment of living, then their completion would mean an end to living. If Tom's view, stated early in the play—that books should be used for their learning and then thrown away before one is trapped in their conspicuous covers—is to emerge victorious, then the bookshelves must fall down. That Shepard has them do so in hilarious fashion and by sleight of play-writing hand is a tribute to his craft. The improbability of his nebulous plot never distracts the viewer from the unity of his vision.

At the end of the short play, the characters engage in a discussion of the constitution of an ideal city. From the construction of book-shelves, which represent the intimate aspect of family life, that is, the private unit of family, Shepard moves onto the city, the most advanced form of living, an aspect of life that demands an allegiance of community over privacy. Shepard had been reading studies of city planning during the construction of this play and had become fascinated with architecture as a tool of philosophy. In the coda at the end of the play, Mom and Pop talk about their ideal city and how it might be built. As they speak their lines, they appear to be reading them from a book. The inference may be that Mom and Pop are still tied to book as affectation and life as image, though Shepard remains vaguely wily on this point. While they are speaking their lines, Tom, Donna, and Ed are taking down all the bookshelves that have been put in place. On this point the text, and texture, seems ingrained: the characters either know the architectural plans won't work—the bookshelves cannot, by the nature of their frag-mented isolation, house an idea of community though they may be able to store various communities of ideas. Possibly the characters are afraid to risk their dream of an ideal construct and find their realization wanting. Yet, in not completing the edifice of the book-shelves, they have kept their dream alive; unfulfilled, the dream remains viable. The architecture of their lives goes on unfinished, but it goes on.

Shepard's first full-length play, and his first work with more than one setting, *La Turista,* was produced at American Place Theatre on March 4, 1967, with a cast that included Sam Waterston as the male protagonist and Joyce Aaron as the female lead; the director was Jacques Levy. Shepard had insisted that no reviewers be per-mitted to write on the work, since the play was part of a works-in-progress series and therefore should be free of the pressures of journal criticism. The distinguished critic and writer, Elizabeth

Hardwick, then married to Robert Lowell, whose play *The Old Glory* had also been produced in the theater series, decided to break the ban. Her review, published in the *New York Review of Books,* of which she was (and remains) an editor, hailed the young Shepard as "one of the three or four gifted playwrights alive." Ever the man of contraries, Shepard used Hardwick's review as part of his application for a Guggenheim grant. He got it.

Like his earlier work, the play is loosely based on his experiences, in this case on the vacation he took with Aaron in Mexico on cheap buses and in some flea-infested hotels. As a result of an appalling airplane trip, with plane conditions and weather contributing to a stew of near-hysteria, Shepard vowed never to fly again. He and Aaron returned from Mexico to New York by bus, a three-day trip at minimum. (Shepard's reputation as a nonflyer has now become a show-biz legend, and it is interesting to speculate that in his rejection of this one means of transport, Shepard may be engaging in another, and this time covert, rejection of the father who soared patriotically through the skies during World War II.) In the play Shepard also transforms the plane experience into the dreaded tourist disease, dysentery. The premise of a vacation becomes the starting point for a dramatic encounter between two types of civilization, two periods of history, and two widely disparate kinds of people and consciousness. On the surface of act 1, Shepard lumps his expressionistic extremes of consciousness into two labels: the blank, sun-worshiping American tourist and the impenetrable primitive Mexican. He then plays one group off against another. As the act opens, Kent and Salem are in their hotel room on their single beds, with Kent ready to rush off to the toilet to deal with his dysentery (*La Turista* in tourist parlance). Kent and Salem are bright yuppie types (though the phrase was unknown at that time); their white skins have been turned bright orange as a result of their unthinking sun worship: they are paying the price for their refusal to think beyond stereotypes. If Mexico is the land of the sun vacation, they will have sun, no matter what its other inheritances. If Mexico is the wonderful cheap vacationland their tourist agents and their own fantasies have promised them, they will have such a vacation no matter what it costs.

Kent and Salem are Shepard's portrait of intelligent ninnies, people without values except for status and label. When they are forced into real contact with people and things they have until this time manipulated according to their fantasies, they are thrown back across crumbling defense lines. Living in fantasy, which is what their "real world" has become, they cannot deal with the "real world" when their fantasies enter into the room and demand the game be played out. Like monsters of the imagination, the fantastic shapes take over, given half a recreation.

Everything about Kent and Salem is neon, plastic, disposable. Their opening conversation sets the scene: they are discussing the origins of sunburn in a manner that reveals their unused, disposable intelligence. Kent explains that the red color of sunburn is a defense by the body system, or blood, to repair skin damage. Salem sums up Kent's explanation as a scientific fact that does not capture the "magic" of the problem. Magic is what Salem is after, but self-indulgent fantasy is a more accurate term for her explanations of reality. Later in the play, real magic will appear in the form of primitive rite and ritual, a magic that will defeat Kent and Salem, inflicting death on one and paranoid whimpering on the other. Kent and Salem's names reflect, as well, their lack of substance: they are cigarette puffs blown away by any strong exhilaration of passion, as the smouldering utterances of the Mexican boy who comes into their room will demonstrate.

It is interesting to compare Shepard's prose poem in *Motel Chronicles* with Kent and Salem, who got their names from cigarette brands. In the Shepard prose poem, Shepard's father refuses Shepard's gift of a carton of Old Gold cigarettes. He keeps instead a can of butts in an old Yuban coffee can; he unravels and threads together a butt or butts into a new cigarette each time he wishes to smoke. Shepard's father makes a real cigarette out of what grows in his container; he wastes nothing. Thus, Shepard's father's cigarette becomes a homage to the American tradition of self-reliance in contrast to the mass-manufactured product of an impersonal, acquisitive age. By itself, Shepard's prose poem seems a dedication to his father's Yankee miserliness issuing into practicality, and into a widening eccentricity—it is easier, after all, to buy a pack of cigarettes (or, better, to receive a gift of a carton of them) than to roll one's own. Eccentricity is, however, at the least, unique; it cannot be massively manufactured or produced on consignment. To hold onto one's eccentricity is to be stubborn about one's presumed identity; to keep on with the practices of one's eccentricity is to refuse to yield to pressures of social conformity. For Shepard, who sees and portrays the world in striking and conflicting images, the eccentric is a glory, while the average may turn out to be nothing more than mean. In Greece, the mean might have been golden, but as Shepard sees it, the mean has become a tarnished brassy muddle.

Shepard in his prose poem is praising the personal, the self-involved response, even to the point of a lowly cigarette, while he is portraying Kent and Salem as meaningless creatures who have rationalized away their substance under the prevailing guise of acquisitive consumerism. Their insubstantiality insures their defeat against the rigidly stubborn world of ritual, a world they mistakenly believe they can compartmentalize into a tourist experience.

Sitting on their beds like sunburst flowers, Kent and Salem have just about finished their analyses of sunburn when the door to their room opens, and a dark boy or young man (his age is indeterminate in Shepard's script) enters. Kent dives under the bedsheet, but Salem is more adventurous: this kind of fantasy is *her* fantasy (the boy is attractive). Weak as he is from dysentery, Kent tries to phone the hotel manager, but the boy rips out the phone cord. When Kent, trying still to appear the Master of the Situation, orders the boy to leave the room, the boy spits at him. Horrified, Kent rushes into the bathroom to cleanse himself. Salem speaks to the boy, telling a story of her youth. When she was ten years old she went to a county fair with her family. The family returned home at night, and for some reason she spit on the top step leading to the house just as the father was stepping onto it. She felt an irresistible urge to do so, she tells the boy. Though she does not make an explicit parallel with the boy's spit and her own, the connection is apparent to her and to the audience. As she finishes her story, the phone rings (the same phone whose cord had been ripped apart by the boy moments before). The boy answers it, saying in English to the caller, "How did you know where I was?" He places the receiver back on the hook and addresses Salem as Mom. He tells her the story of his youth, when a group of American ranchers came into his Mexican town and killed his father and stole his sisters and brothers to work in the fields for twelve hours a day. The story is a cliché analogue of colonial exploitation, and Shepard's language is ironically sentimental and yet filled with its own pathos. The admixture of language creates an uneasy mood.

History having exploited him, the boy now decides to exploit his situation. Having been materialized by the tourists' fantasy, he takes command of the narrative and climbs into Kent's bed. He tells Salem as he does so that he was once in the movies; he served the needs of a macho movie director, who treated him like a serf. At this point Kent has returned from the bathroom, dressed like a honcho cowboy, with a Western hat, plaid shirt, shiny boots, and pistols dangling from his belt. He is missing one part of attire: pants. He struts around with only the upper part of him resplendent, while the lower part reveals a cowboy emperor in underwear. The "Master" of colonialism, or of the Situation, is thus mimicked in Shepard's costuming of Kent, but Kent does not see himself as others see him. He continues to assert his authority, saying he is now cured of his dysentery, and that the trial of the disease has made him a new, and better, man. He ventilates into a diatribe against the North American obsession with cleanliness; he claims that Americans have become weakened physically by their refusal to live with germs the way that primitive Mexican society accepts them. Having perorated on his new passion, Kent looks to his bed, and finds the Mexican boy there. Kent faints away.

Distraught, Salem phones the hotel doctor on the same phone whose cord has been ripped from the wall. As she ministers to Kent, the boy begins talking like the Kent of the first scene in the play, even to the point of discussing Kent's and Salem's egg-white solution to the dysentery problem. Enter into the room a witch doctor and his son, who perform rites on Kent. While they are performing their rituals, the boy explains the rites to Salem. He is becoming her guide to primitive Indian lore. Suddenly Salem discovers she is a victim of dysentery. She runs into the toilet, and when she returns shortly, her vivid sunburn has been drained away. She exhibits a change of mood, telling the boy to leave the room. The boy refuses, claiming that Salem will need him now. Salem in her turn yanks him offstage and drags him literally up the aisle of the theater, auctioning him off as a laborer of many talents. Look at his body, she implores the audience.

When the phone rings, the boy rushes to answer it. It is his father. They converse in Spanish. The boy agrees to meet his father in some place down some road in the dark of this same night. He turns to Salem, telling her as he leaves, that he and his father will meet and kiss each other and then each will move on in the middle of the night onto different roads. Salem doesn't believe him, and taunts him: "You'll never make it alive."

The extraordinary effects in act 1 of echoing images, the use of stagecraft to suggest a slave sale, the rites of magic performed over a confused, dying, dead body (all three at different times) make *La Turista* a compelling progression of intensity. The audience is not sure if Kent has died in act 1, if the witch doctor and his son are performing a ritual over the dead, or if they are bringing him back from the living. The Mexican boy refers to Kent as dead, but he also refers to Salem as dead. The physical state of Kent and Salem thus becomes protean; their names, signifying smoke, are apt descriptions of their bodies and their psyches. They are dead matter, alien culture, in a civilization of ashes.

But the play is not over. Shepard rewrote the second act entirely when the play was already in rehearsal because he found it wanting. The new second act, and the one in the standard text of the play, opens with a parallel Kent and Salem in an earlier age: this time the signs are in English, the walls are white and not orange, and plastic reigns everywhere, not a serape in sight. The doctor, dressed in a Civil War uniform, and his son, dressed like him but without pistols in his belt, arrive to treat Kent, who is gravely ill. Kent is asleep, and the doctor and his son walk him around the room. They must wake him up, or else the sleeping sickness will kill him, they tell Salem. Kent awakens, but he is not sure what is being done to him.

In this second act the phone is supposedly not in working order, and such a fact suggests that Kent and Salem have no means of obtaining help from their trapped situation. Kent demands to be allowed to leave (he has awakened sufficiently to display some strength); he threatens the doctor. The doctor in turn threatens Kent, and in the bargain, accuses Kent of lack of moral fiber and of unpatriotic bent. Shepard purposefully is mystifying the audience in act 2 by not letting viewers know if the doctor is a villain or a medical benefactor. Kent has become hysterical by this time, and he begins ranting about a beast fleeing from his captors. The doctor attempts to calm him down, but Kent's anxiety is so immense that he runs across the room in flight from what he suggests is a Dr. Frankenstein. As in *Frankenstein* the victim-monster Kent is mortally terrorized that the evil doctor will draw him back into his fold, into the laboratory of his morality. Kent jumps over the doctor and crashes through a screen. He leaves behind only a silhouette of himself, an empty form. Possibly he has escaped; possibly he has killed himself; possibly he has become a raging whimpering victim whose monstrous form will not permit him any sympathy.

Some things are clear about *La Turista*. It is a satire on plastic people. It is a sympathetic treatment of mistreated Mexicans; it is an exposure of social prejudice. What is not eminently clear are the uses to which the mythic elements are put: the witch doctor in act 1 and the doctor in act 2 are creatures whose mysteries are not illuminated through their darkness. Are they healers or fakes? They are shamans, showmen calling on magic to restore, if not to health, then to some kind of order. Is Shepard convinced of their efficacy?

He doesn't say, but the cry to the nonrational, the mysterious, the primitive, makes itself heard through his pages. Shepard is appealing to the mythic and subconscious to provide some way out of the morass into which his deracinated, blanched characters have fallen. He ends his play with Kent's flight and fall. As the doctor says in the second act, he is not interested in how the facts stack up, but in how he can get out of this situation and move into another story. Shepard's doctor in act 2 tells his son, who is objecting to possible inaccuracies in the father's "stories," that "how it went is no concern of mine or yours. All I want to do is finish up and go home." His remark is not merely a laugh getter—it is a plea to leave the past behind him, to go beyond details that may assess past responsibility but do not pay any address to present alternatives. At this point, in the play and in Shepard's evolving view of life, Shepard seems to want to transcend the past by fleeing it. Later, in his family plays, he will realize that only by journeying through it, in the immediacy of recollection, will he be able to move forward.

4

The Plays: 1967–1969

The year 1967 was one of Shepard's most productive years. In addition to *La Turista,* he wrote *Melodrama Play,* which won an Obie Award given by the *Village Voice* for distinguished drama of that year. He wrote a new version of the lost script of his first play, *Cowboys,* which he entitled in disarming honesty, *Cowboys No. 2. Forensic and the Navigators* was put on at Theater Genesis in December of that year, and it went on to win another Obie Award for Shepard (three years later it was revived at Astor Place Theatre on a double bill with Shepard's other science-fiction play, *The Unseen Hand*). Shepard received some financial comfort during the year as well: he was awarded a Rockefeller Foundation grant; the following year he got a Guggenheim grant. Bobbs-Merrill published his collection of plays that year as well.

The year was also important in his personal life. He and Aaron split up though they remained friends. Shepard began dating a new girl, Nancy, with whom he shared an apartment in New York; the other tenant was Bill Hart. That summer he was living in Stroudsburg, Pennsylvania, where he was working as an actor in the Theater Genesis production of a play written by his friend Murray Mednick. He met O-lan Johnson and her mother, Scarlett, who were also connected with the production. O-lan was dating the director, Tony Barsha, but it became apparent to Barsha and Nancy that their mates had discovered a greater passion. Shepard married O-lan two years later, on November 9, 1969 (the month of his birth) at St. Marks Church in the Bowery. The church was the home for Theater Genesis. O-lan was several months pregnant; in 1970 their son, Jesse Mojo, was born.

The focus of *Cowboys No. 2* is on two young urban cowboys trying to keep in touch with the elements and forces that have given them their vision of fortitude. Their talk is about the weather: rain, dark clouds, mud, and floods are what they gather into quasi-philosophic commentary. They talk of the cowboy myth (though they do not use any abstractions in their speech): how they have fought off Indians and saved America, and how their hard life in the open air has made them aware of the value of buddies: they want to remain buddies for life with their buddies. One of them, Chet, has a monologue about the lack of attention given to the filthiness of peacocks, whereas, in contrast, every adult in America seems to comment on the dirtiness of cowboys. Chet proclaims his love of dirt—good-man and good-boy dirt, good sweat, the sweat of vitality. For Chet, *how sweat it is* is preferable to the bourgeois hypocrisy of *how sweet it is*. Chet continues into a passionate description of food, and his passion for it; like sex, food for Chet is to be slobbered over in order to be enjoyed.

Appropriately, Chet's ecstatic monologue ends with a paean to the sun, the sun that is a friend of the cowboy and watches out for him. Only, as Chet ends his monologue, he cannot find his friend Stu. Chet exits into the audience looking for Stu, but, as if knowing he is already a relic—a man believing in a lost mythos, a wordsmith whose words are walling up his vision—he degeneratively ages into an old man. By the time he has reached the orchestra seats in his search for his buddy, he *is* an old man. In Shepard the figure of the Old Man is a signifier of his lament for an age fled, for the disappearance of the Western mythos from modern American culture.

During Chet's monologue, another duet, identified only as Man #1 and Man #2, who had been at the sides of the stage from the beginning of the play, have walked onto the center of the stage. They begin talking of the city; their talk has no beginning and no ending: it is a refrain, a litany, an endless string of petty matters, like the cost of rent for their apartment and the choice of menu for their dinner. While their conversation is loaded with numbers (even their names are numbers), their speech lacks any commitment to *figures* of speech. They find Stu, who is asleep, and wake him up. For some reason they call him Mel. (It is interesting that Stu is Stu in the beginning of this play, for Stu is also the man who ends up in the bathtub in *Chicago*. Thus Stu has progressed, or regressed, from the cowboy to the tub dweller, from the cowboy announcing his challenges to the outside world to the urban caveman sinking into a walled, airless shelter.)

As a parallel to the sun of Chet, who is a friend to cowboys, the sun of Man #1 and Man #2 is a dreary stunted circle of little light. In the mouths of these urban automatons even the sun becomes prosaic, lacking in any high noon of brilliance, except for the two men's final reference to vultures. For vultures are a part of the sun of these two men, and they predict dire times for Stu and Chet, who have not made any preparation for shade. Walking offstage and then again onstage in the uniform of dull business clothes—again Shepard indulges in his love for costume as sign of meaning—the two men begin lipreading from scripts they have opened and placed in front of themselves. Their talk is ordered, willed, constrained. Unlike Stu and Chet, they have no spontaneity. The image of these two men reading is the final image of the play, and it is in its way more frightening than Shepard's resort to apocalypse. For these two men make a monotone of everything—all fun is drained from the life they present as that lived by most of middle-class America.

The fun-and-games motif of mistaken identity may be seen throughout Shepard's work in the guise of role-playing and monologues of fantasia. In *Melodrama Play,* a one-act "melodrama with music," first produced at La Mama ETC on May 18, 1967, under the direction of Tom O'Horgan, Duke, a popular rock star, has had one big hit, but hasn't produced a new hit in a long time. As the play opens, he's trying out new songs. The lyrics are comments on his conflicts and yearning. The first song is about the pressure he feels of everyone on his back—his exploiters, his friends, his conscience. Duke's split between his desire for the pleasures of a simple life—a good sexual companion and security from economic worries—and the pleasures of fame, with its complex demands, is exemplified in his songs. His girlfriend, the sexy Dana in jeans, leather jacket, "shades, etc.," doesn't understand his words. She says she just loves Duke, that is, up to the point he measures up to the royalty of rock imagism in her mind. She is finally convinced of his perfidy when he asks her to buy him a black suit, white shirt, tie, and black shoes. Such a change in image is too much for Dana's Rock iconography, and she flings back at Duke the money he has pressed into her hands.

Duke's split also is exemplified in the setting—two photographs, one of Robert Goulet and the other of Bob Dylan, both without eyes. The symbolism is apparent in that Duke cannot see through them or into them; if his idols are blind, he is too. Thus he must come to his inner sight, he must become himself. At the moment however he is adrift in the space between each of them as role models—the bohemian free spirit and the conventional, good-looking talented romantic Middle America exemplum (Goulet was born in Montreal of French-Canadian stock, but Shepard is right in using him as an American good-boy phenomenon). Duke's quandary will be further dramatized in his decision to cut his long hair, and to attempt to buy a black suit, a white shirt, and shiny black shoes. The attempt represents Duke's desperate lunge at finding himself by going back to what he once was, when he had only *one* image to sustain and impel him forward: the Goulet, middle-American, short-hair vision of the good life. By becoming a rock songwriter, by letting his hair grow long, he has let "it" all out—though, paradoxically, something is hidden and never let out of Duke. That resolute inability to let go of whatever it is that binds him to his past is the crux of the play.

Duke paints his dilemma in a long monologue to Peter, the "guard" and assistant to Duke's manager Floyd. Duke explains that he, Duke, stole his brother's song and thus became famous and rich, and earned the admiration of those "closest to his heart." The paradox is that the self-knowledge he gained by his theft is destroying him because he cannot drop his old self or move to his newer self. The newer self—the self exemplified in the wandering, anarchic image of (Bob) Dylan—is not what he wants, not exclusively at any rate, but what he feels he is being dragged into. Duke, in essence, is at the crossroads of a new world in which fame and bohemianism are waiting to welcome him, but he cannot let go of his earlier senses of responsibility: he still refuses to leave behind the world of ordinary responsibility typified by a white shirt and a black suit.

Ironically, the song that Duke has appropriated from his brother Drake is a rousing ballad to break free of one's confinement. The "prisoner," the song says, does not have to lie in the bed he has made by his passivity; he can be free if he will act on his will to freedom. Yet Duke, his brother Drake who wrote the song, and Cisco, their piano-playing colleague, will not have the courage to break free, to rise out of the bed that is their prison.

In the course of the plot Duke's brother Drake is assumed to be the great songwriter of the hit tune that Duke has supposedly written (which in truth he is, since Duke stole it from him). Now that Drake is believed to be Duke, the man who wrote the song is the man who wrote the song though he is not the man credited with writing the song. Duke confesses at this point to his guard Peter that at last he feels free to be himself, but Peter, the literal guard and the metaphorical guardian of Duke, rejects the confession as a "lie." It is a plea, Peter admits, but he, Peter, is not going to fall for it just because of its "simplicity." The "sincerity" of it masks the real truth, Peter says, which is that Duke has been living out a lie, or a self-deception. He has been running from himself all his life, and Peter, the jailhouse/company guard/warden is going to put a stop to all that permissiveness. Peter will club both Duke and Drake as each attempts to cross the threshold of his Faustian prison room.

The elements of *Melodrama Play* will resurface in *A Lie of the Mind* almost two decades later, particularly in the use of the brother motif and in their punitive treatment on stage. Duke and his brother Drake are forced to crawl on all four legs; they are reduced to infants and animals, helpless and squeaking but fine as long as they obey the authority of parental, law-giving commands. In *A Lie of the Mind* Jake is made to behave like a trained dog; in *Melodrama Play* Duke paces furiously like a dog trying to please his master but confused by commands he cannot fathom. Peter also has a monologue in which he tells of an incident that took place when he was sixteen years old, just after he arrived in a "huge" city. In his monologue Peter says a creature on all fours pursued him; Peter ran off to dodge the animal, but the creature followed him, and catching up to him, told Peter to read the dog tag round his neck. The tag read, simply: "Arizona." The man/dog asked for directions to that place. Peter watched the creature scamper off and then Peter felt the hands of a mighty force on his shoulder. They were the hands of a policeman; those hands took Peter through a dark alley into a house of dark correction, where Peter was told to take off his pants. The monologue is interrupted at this point—but the import is clear. Peter is being punished for sending the dog/man off to Arizona. The punishment will be a whipping, the whipping, as Peter reveals in the way he tells his story, becomes both a feared consequence and one anticipated with pleasure. The whipping absolves the sin and allows for the necessary release of the sin/pressure/pain syndrome. Later in the play Peter will take off his pants and strut around pants-less, an automaton of planned discipline response. The image is chilling (and again prescient of the incident in *A Lie of the Mind* in which Jake, clad only in his underwear and an American flag, runs off from his mother's home in Los Angeles all the way to Montana to see his wife whom he earlier had beaten nearly to death). The imagery becomes revelatory when it is remembered that Shepard's father ran off to Arizona and the desert because he could not stand the pressures of middle-class/suburban demands. Phoenix is the place of Duke's next concert—he must have a song for it. Thus Arizona is layered in the imagery of quest and rejection, of goal and retreat.

By these expressionistic means of manic monologues, character asides to his audience, and choral commentary—a band, suspended in a cage from the ceiling comes down to sing two songs serving as thematic emphases—Shepard is treating his primal theme: self-knowledge. By exciting these images into the reader's limning awareness, Shepard is suggesting several vital concerns about freedom, discipline, and self-expression. Perhaps the one most vital to him is the relationship to his father, who both "disciplined" and beat him with one hand and inspired love and admiration with the other. The sound of one hand clapping was also the sound of the other hand zapping him. Shepard's pain was the outcome of the father's neurotic conflicts, a pain that continued to reverberate in Shepard's imaginative constructs long after the son left home, a pain that divided his world between adult responsibilities and adolescent yearnings for the privacy of a world without pain. That pain becomes the world of his drama in a hundredfold different and inventive disguises at learning the truth about his world.

A subplot, or rather a side ploy to the main concern of the play, lies in Shepard's by now customary diatribe against intellectuals, or at least in his view, intellectual parasites. The animus against such intellectual parasites opens and closes the "melodrama." This time the parasite is a sociology professor who is writing a paper on Duke and the creative mind. The professor has written a letter with a series of inane (as Shepard presents them) questions about the creative process. Duke reacts with his customary pique to such pretentiousness by folding the letter into a paper airplane and flying it out to the audience. The incident becomes a means for Shepard to write several witty comments about writing and its interpretation by different critics and different critical structures and terminology. Shepard has Duke's girlfriend Dana, for example, and later the manager, Floyd, scold Duke for his thoughtless action. They claim the letter can be used by anyone who picks it up as a card of identity. The implication is that identity in this play can be assumed without much depth or test of veracity. Identity is a transient role, a piece of officially threaded paper rather than an immaterial substance of spiritual fibers. The questions that the sociology professor, Damon, has put to Duke become profoundly ironic: since role-playing in America is the most popular current fashion of identity, any change in status mandates a change in identity. The artist then does not lead society or show society his vision and by that gift provide an alternative to contemporary fashion. Instead, the artist becomes a plaything of his society, a pathetic imitator and whiner trying to discover new tricks to please an old master. Just such a view of Drake, pacing furiously on all fours, is seen as Damon's interview with Duke is heard on the radio, an interview that was never given, but that fact is beside the point in a world given to identity by professorial-rationalized authority. And yet perhaps it is not beside the point, for the Duke who has been interviewed on the radio is society's manifested wish to have a Duke interviewed on the radio. The phantom is as solid a consciousness as the unmanageable flesh-and-blood image.

Melodrama Play thus continues old themes and initiates new versions of them. Brother against brother, brother for brother; the fearsome disciplinarian who is a victim himself; the animus against authority, whether in the deviously unctuous Professor of Sociology or the openly crass managers willing to imprison and torture an artist until he produces something for his next concert (or movie or theater play); and in the divided hero, spurred by a desire for fame and a desire for the ease of anonymity; the artist's role in society and his opposing desires between free will, free expression, and fear of ostracism.

Forensic and the Navigators, produced at Theater Genesis on December 29, 1967, under the direction of Ralph Cook, with O-lan Johnson playing the role of Oolan, is an expressionistic play in which name tags do shed some light and identification on the characters and on the content of the play. Forensic is a character debating within himself the roles he must play—in life, in society, in personal and social relationships. As the play opens he is writing on a notepad with his pen—the allusion to Shepard's well-observed penchant for writing notes on a pad he kept in his shirt pocket is a part of the subtext (Shepard wrote in longhand). Forensic's friend Emmet is typing, presumably a story because Forensic asks Emmet, what's the "story so far?" Forensic wants to know when they're going to cut out of the place, just as the doctor in *La Turista* wanted to know "when they were getting out of the place" (the play). This element of a play being written about a play being written is emphasized throughout; it is, like all of Shepard's work, a part of the play everyone is having with each other. Characters make references to the process of writing and creating. These same characters comment on the difficulties of living their lives as characters in a personal and mythic drama that only is partly about them. Also, and peculiar to this play, is the comic motif of Rice Krispies as an American tonic that will make one strong and able to fight off the evil intruders from any outside world—the "outside," as in *4-H Club* and *Chicago,* being the world beyond the apartment in which the protagonists dwell.

The third member of the group is Oolan, the buddies' girlfriend. (The three characters are based on Shepard, Bill Hart, and a composite of O-lan Johnson and Shepard's former girlfriend, Nancy). Oolan is ordered to the kitchen to get the "boys" breakfast, specifically Rice Krispies, while the men continue with their work (in this case, the cowboys are writing). While she is doing her motherly duties, two exterminators arrive at the front door. They have orders to "bomb" the place. Forensic and Emmet hide under the table, while Oolan attempt to dissuade the exterminators from their foul project. The exterminators resist her entreaty because they know they are in the right place for their job: the position of the table in the room identifies it as the sore spot to be exterminated. There is no getting away from the fact: the table fits into their kit of association, and therefore they cannot be mistaken about their judgment of guilt by association. Emmet and Forensic in the meantime are hiding under the table, as if running under cover, another associational piece of convicting evidence to the exterminators. All the comic, outlandish allusions suggest that Shepard is mocking a historic period's ethos of sentencing people on appearance and prejudgment, just as long hair identified the rebel-outcast in his high-school Duarte days or an alternative life-style identified the bohemian who lived in a Lower East Side tenement flat and worked in off-off-Broadway theaters.

When, for some mysterious reason, the exterminators believe the table has moved—though in the stage directions the table is said to be in the same place it always was—the exterminators begin to question if they are in the right place. As in *Fourteen Hundred Thousand,* position is all-important: in the earlier play, a mother's reverie about snow became the buildup to snow as a backdrop for a house library; in *Forensic* the table as content of subversion by its position on the floor becomes the determinant of consciousness. After the second exterminator leaves to make a phone call to his superiors, the first exterminator becomes concerned about Oolan, who has fainted. In typical high-school melodramatic fashion, this first exterminator, the man who has stayed behind, falls in love with his captive beauty, or rather with his image of her. (The high-school aura runs throughout the play, with references to "lettermen," leather jackets, hairstyles among the teenies.) He holds the unconscious girl in his arms and describes his love for her in idealized romantic language.

Emmet and Forensic utilize the time that the exterminator is using to recite his love to the unhearing Oolan: they steal from the distracted man his gun and gas mask and take him prisoner. By this time Oolan has revived, and Emmet orders her to bring him his Rice Krispies. Over the repast of the Rice Krispies, the four occupants of the apartment become involved in discussions of the headquarters of the fort of the exterminators, and how such a fort might be attacked and captured. The first exterminator is willing to betray his organization and tell all if Oolan is given to him in exchange. Forensic is willing to sell Oolan, but Emmet has qualms. He recites a long list of sufferings that Oolan has already endured when she was sold down the river in her journey through life. The allusions are clear and hackneyed awarenesses of woman's victimizations, but the details are hazy, possibly because Shepard was expressing sympathy without depth of commitment.

While the issue of Oolan's fate is being disputed, the second exterminator returns. He tells the four characters to clear out of the apartment because the exterminators are coming. It is too late to stop them. When the first exterminator declares his love for Oolan, the second exterminator responds with an announcement of betrayal. He begins a long monologue about the difficulties of his job and of his position, and he complains bitterly about the lack of sympathy and understanding he deserves for the dangerous mission to which he has remained faithful. The play ends as smoke fills the stage: all five characters are being gassed, and there is no way out.

Shepard's play expresses the paranoia of the young and anti-Establishment figures of the 1960s: this was the time of the Weathermen and underground protest activities, and the mass attack on them by government forces and the lack of understanding of their idealism by the majority of Americans. Oolan, Forensic, and Emmet become picked for extermination because they do not fit into the neat California highway patrolmen's uniforms of vision (the stage directions explicitly call for California patrol uniforms for the exterminators, though the description of the tenement apartment is unmistakably Lower East Side of New York nostalgia). At the same time the exterminators are treated in a sympathetic fashion—the first exterminator is a sweet guy who falls romantically in love with Oolan, the second is a seemingly disciplined worker threatened by lack of authority figures. What is evident in this play is that all the characters are, at one time or another, referred to as Forensic. The device is meant to make the audience aware that each of the characters is debating within himself the kind of character he is. In stage terms, each of the characters is trying to identify the role he is being asked to play. Each is involved in a forensic activity about the meaning of character. That all the characters should end up being gassed represents Shepard's bitter comment on an impersonal society.

Shepard's play is reflective on the double life he often portrays and treats in his work—the world of the rebel and the world of the conformist, the traditional and the anarchic, the conventional and the individualistic. In this play the roles are interchanged between the exterminators and the apartment dwellers: all get gassed because each has a spark of the socially undesirable. Shepard also uses the brother/antibrother configuration that will become such a profound part of his later work. In effect he prestages *True West* in the opening scenes of this play when he has Emmet and Forensic sitting and writing, one at a typewriter, the other on a notepad, just as the brothers Lee and Austin enact the process of writing, and coming to terms with their feelings, in *True West.* Although Emmet and Forensic differ from each other, they are not hostile to each other as in the later plays in which brother is pitted against brother in a family Civil War. In *Forensic and the Navigators* Emmet and Forensic are brothers who do not go to war over the fate of their Oolan of Troy; their odyssey has roots in an American Western comedy rather than in ancient Greek myth.

In 1968 Shepard turned down an opportunity to work with Arlo Guthrie on the script of *Alice's Restaurant* when the noted Italian director Michelangelo Antonioni asked him to write the script for *Zabriskie Point,* to be produced by MGM Pictures. Shepard was treated in high style while in Rome, but he and the famed director could not agree on Shepard's script. Antonioni wanted to create a politically oriented film, and Shepard refused to put modish anti-American diatribes into the mouths of the film's leading characters. Shepard's abortive film project was followed by another: while in Rome he was asked to write a film script for one of his idols—Mick Jagger—and the Rolling Stones. He moved to Keith Richards's estate in England to work on the script, but the production, which bore the name *Maxagasm,* was canceled by the sudden death of Rolling Stones guitarist Brian Jones. Shepard's agent, Toby Cole, who was devoted to him (she also promoted the work of several now-prominent off-Broadway writers), was trying to arrange a Broadway production, but her deal fell through. Shepard did work on one film project that got finished, a low-budget film he wrote with Robert Frank, *Me and My Brother*. He also worked anonymously as a staff writer in Hollywood.

During this period Shepard was still suffering from the states of aftershock of his family history and from the pressures of his now high-powered career. His relationship with his father was to continue to be the most impinging dramatic force in his life, and his brushes with luxury and a high style of living, with all its lures of decadence, would afford him little ease. *The Holy Ghostly* is his most direct confrontation with the father-son theme, though it may not be his most overt facing of the conflict. It was produced first on a La Mama European tour in 1969 and then brought to the McCarter Theater in Princeton, New Jersey, in January 1974 by the New Troupe Company. Both productions were directed by Tom O'Horgan. In the short play, a father given the generic name of Pop, and his son, Ice, given a symbolic name to represent in the father's view the eternal coldness and ingratitude of children, are sitting alone in the desert, where the father now lives. The father has opted out of the rat race for another life as a desert rat, but he fears his mortality, and he has taken to phoning his son in New York, a successful rock star, and to pleading with his son to come and chase away the death spirits.

As the play opens, Ice is toasting marshmallows the way his father likes them. (In *The Rock Garden* the father toasted the marshmallows and salt crackers sometimes all night over an open fire because he liked them so much; in performing his toasting, Ice is enacting a form of homage to his father.) Ice justifies his name by saying he represents one of two forces in the universe, the sun and the ice, and that ice is now the dominant force. At the end of the play the father will introduce a third force, fire, as he throws his own corpse into the fire to have it consumed, and perhaps to start fresh with a new body. The polar forces—sun, ice, and fire—are complemented by the forces of an Indian spirit-god, the Chindi, whose deep knowledge allows for vision beyond life and death, and who tells the still-living father that he, the father, has already died; in addition, there is an Indian witch, Chindi's Ole Lady, with her own supernatural powers.

When the father complains that Ice doesn't care about him, Ice points out that he dropped everything in response to his father's phone call and came out to the Arizona desert to see him. The father disputes Ice's success in New York and constantly refers to his son's betrayal in changing his family name for that of a rock moniker. The father is Stanley Hewitt Moss the Sixth, and Ice is Stanley Hewitt Moss the Seventh, but the son has become all ice—cold and ungrateful enough to reject his family identity.

While the father and son are debating their heritage, the spirit of Chindi manifests itself, and Ice, in fear of the Chindi, runs offstage. The spirit declares the father's body a dead one and adds that the father must now move on to another sphere; the spirit points to a corpse on stage that he proclaims the father's dead body. The father denies his own death—he clings to life and to his fierce desire to shape the world in his image. Chindi runs off when the father begins to shoot at him.

As Ice returns onstage, the father accuses him of having masqueraded as the Chindi. He begins a long harangue about the son's faults, the son's rejection of the values the father has tried to instill in him for eighteen years. The father accuses the son of lacking discipline, of being a "sissy," of having effeminate traits (the father makes a reference to his son's makeup, though there is no indication that Ice wears makeup. Most likely the reference is a telescoped allusion to the makeup Ice must wear on stage as a rock performer, and to the world of show-biz–make-believe). When Ice reacts in cold anger, threatening to kill his father if he keeps on with the torturous charges, the father calls Ice by the name he gave him at his birth, Stanley, and asks him to be "kind." The witch enters at this point and warns the father that he is a ghost. She tells him he is on earth only to finish up his last-minute business and to get himself in good shape for eternity. When the witch leaves, Ice and his father speak more temperately, but it is at this point that Ice tells his story of the elements of fire and ice. The sun and the ice were the two forces in the cosmos millions of years ago, but in a collision, some of the ice's crust got into the sun's belly, and years later those pieces of ice melted. The ensuing steam pressure caused the sun to explode, and its figments became the planets we know today. The father objects to his son's "fairy tales"; he accuses him again of being a "sissy." Enraged, Ice takes down the gun from the wall and shoots his father, who cries out that he will give everything he has to his son. He pleads only that his son not leave him.

"Yer pa is dying," the father uses as his last snare, but Ice has already deserted him, having walked offstage. Alone, the father justifies his ways, calling his son a sneak and a weasel, someone unable to fight in the old way, the Teddy Roosevelt manner, someone who doesn't appreciate the discipline forged out of epic struggle. The father begins a dance of death in front of the fire he is building. Onto the fire he throws all the things he has accumulated as his defenses through his life: his gun, his sleeping bag and blanket for lone nights in the desert, his radio to shut out human communication, his cans of food to deny the food others might give him in an act of sharing. He declares he will be a changed man, and his son will be proud of him. The play ends with his father saying he is ready for death, but also saying he has never felt better in his life. Shepard thus ends his portrayal of a man who will not come to terms with his shortcomings, or rather will not compromise those terms in order to make peace with his son, by giving to him the paradox of rationalized self-blindness.

The parricide in this play—for Ice believes he has killed his father, and Pop is a dead man in Chindi calculations—is dramatized in comic style, and consequently no shock of horror ensues in the playacting commission of it. Shepard is not after dramatic shock—he is not writing a Greek gasp of tragedy, but an ambivalent comedy of parental clinging and childhood's end. In freeing himself from the world his father imposed on him—the world in which men did certain things and other things were forbidden to them as silly, effeminate, or transsexual—Ice must shoot from the hip in one parting macho shot. The "holy ghostly" is the act of parricide, of killing the thing one loved in the primacy of one's life. Shepard's later plays will show that this parricidal drama did not kill his "holy ghostly."' The inspiration for Shepard's most profound dramas will continue in the presence of Shepard's father figure in them as a memory-ingrained plant of the desert.

Shepard's relationship with his father may also be gleaned in *The Unseen Hand* and in that play's exposure of paternal tyranny. The play is the title work in a collection published in 1986, some fifteen or more years after the composition of the plays in the volume. In a brief introduction to the collection, Shepard wrote that these plays were now plays of another age to him; he wrote that the plays seemed the wanderings of a youthful, confused, searching mind. While Shepard writes that he feels embarrassed at times now by the plays, he does not specify which plays, or the specific content in them, that embarrass him. He admits the plays are a part of the whole of him, but he insists the plays make sense only if seen in historical context, as parts of the theatrical and sociopolitical scene of the 1960s, and as part of his own nature maturing into greater consciousness. The insistence on historical context by Shepard, who otherwise mocks historicism as an evasion of timeless truth, becomes a fascinating context in its own argument, and should at some time be examined for the issues it raises.

First produced at La Mama ETC in New York on December 26, 1969, *The Unseen Hand* is a blend of science fiction, Old Western myth and heroics, and high-school vanities. A totally implausible world is being presented—a world that initially seems one concocted by a flourishing imagination. The admixture of genres and bloodletting of form are typical of youthful rebellion against what is accepted by an older generation as societal restraint for the good of all. Shepard's view, representing the younger generation, sees traditional form and traditional values as an imprisonment of the imagination, but, as is so often the case with Shepard, the immediacy of immaturity gives way to a realization of profound yearning and irreversible, unshatterable insight. The play represents Shepard's conflicts in familiar areas of concern: this time they are science fiction and Western values.

As the play opens, an old Western grizzler—the Gabby Hayes–like hero of Shepard's imagination—climbs out of a dead Chevy. The car has no wheels, but its battered body continues to drive the imagination. The place is Azuza, California, a typical small town in the US, with everything from A to Z. As Shepard presents it, Azuza is a dystopia of the late twentieth century, with mediocrity as its ruling order. The time is an era fueled by scientific totalitarianism; Western humanism has become a museum piece. The archaisms of Blue Morphan, who has climbed out of the dead car, is signaled in his appearance, his manner, and his vision of a good world: they are all part of an age familiar in legend and alien in contemporary context. Blue's *adolescence,* as a chronological adolescent, as a young man, as an old man (he is 120 years old), is made clear from the beginning of the play. He is summed up by his brother, Cisco, who defines Blue's ideals as robbing, raping, and killing, "like in the old times."

What has been developing in America while Blue retreated into a desert coma is a mechanization that has throttled old Western values. That mechanization is represented both by the "space" freak, Willie, who shows up on the scene, and by "The Kid," who represents Shepard's literal adolescent problems of adjustment. Willie is "burned out," a "spaced" freak; the contextual allusions to the 1960s drug scene should be kept in mind, as Shepard insists in his introduction to the collection of plays of which *The Unseen Hand* is a part. Yet Willie (notice his name—Will) also represents a desire for timeless freedom, which exists in all people who want their space, their private sphere of the imagination. Willie relates that the people in Nogoland, his country or sphere of time and space, are allowed freedom within limits: if they stray beyond the prescribed law, the Unseen Hand squeezes their minds till the dangerous elements of rebellious freedom are burned away. Willie has been "burned" several times—the marks can be seen on his body as he talks to the incredulous Blue (dressed appropriately in Western gear). While Willie is telling his story to Blue, The Kid appears on stage from (seemingly) nowhere—he is a high-school cheerleader, kidnapped and gang-beaten by a bunch of rich kids from a rival high school. The Kid is angry—he's always believed in his high school, in the values of small-town America, and now he has been betrayed by those same forces and values. He begs Blue to let him stay with Blue, and Blue, out of compassion, agrees to give him refuge.

At this point Blue's brother, Cisco, materializes. Willie, the space freak, has conjured him and brought him to Azuza. Willie cannot free his people in Nogoland, but he has the power to release some people from their imprisoned spheres. Cisco, and Blue's other brother, Sycamore, who will also rise from the world of the Dead and return to Azuza, are free beings of legend if not in historical verity. Cisco finds, like Rip Van Winkle, that adjustment is a trying task in a new world. He, who always believed in the freedom of the West—the code of the independent loner—now finds such a code extinct in the new world in which he has been brought back to life. Sycamore, who shows up a short time later, also realizes he's out of his Western element in this new world.

For his Promethean daring in materializing Cisco and Sycamore, the space freak Willie has been zonked out by the Unseen Hand—it is his punishment for trespassing on the territory of the gods of science and totalitarianism. When he revives from his shock, he begins to discuss a coup attempt with the three gunslinger brothers against the Unseen Hand. Overhearing them, The Kid becomes furious and accuses the four of being un-American revolutionaries, subversives under their guise of true-blue shearling and Stetson. The historical context can again be presumed here, for The Kid is raising his gun against those who would threaten American values, Azuza high school, and everything out of 1950 conformist beliefs. Yet while The Kid is presented as an angry fool who lives by adolescent shibboleths and by the prejudices of a definite time period, he also clothes an eternal vice: the creature who will rationalize his desires for security into a vigilance against anybody who questions them. Shepard gives The Kid a threefold credo, which The Kid adopts proudly as his banner of admission throughout the world's corridors of vigilante justice: constant movement, absolute mistrust, eternal vigilance.

As Willie moves to subdue The Kid, The Kid shoots at him. The bullets accomplish nothing, neither rupture nor decease, for Willie is space, freedom, immateriality. He is a spirit that cannot be killed by physical aggression. Willie goes into a trance that permits him to invade The Kid's body/being and overpower The Kid. The trance act and its victory over the forces of evil/agression, as represented in The Kid, bring Willie to an awareness of his powers: he realizes that he has discovered the secret weapon against the Unseen Hand and the means to freedom for his people in Nogoland. The Unseen Hand's power of control can be lifted by the will to freedom—what may take time and pain will surely come to pass if spirit and belief sustain themselves.

Willie decides to return to Nogoland to lead a revolution. Blue, Cisco, and Sycamore—the three brothers from the Old West—are left on stage, along with The Kid, who is paralyzed in fear and trembling from his pain. Sycamore wants to kill The Kid because The Kid is capable of betraying them again (this time for being outside the law as Western gunslingers of Old). Blue dissuades him, asserting that killing The Kid doesn't resolve the problem of the outlaw dissident; it only brings on more restraining orders. Blue decides to go off *somewhere,* to a desert outpost, a place where he can feel free. Cisco asks to join him. Both feel young again and do somersaults in the air; their sense of freedom has been revived, and thy do not want to be imprisoned by the good/bad offices of modern technology, as the creatures of Nogoland were/are. Only Sycamore remains in Azuza, deciding he's had enough of roaming. He's going to "stay awhile."

As Sycamore is left alone on stage, with a mute Kid, he begins to age into an old man. The youth of his body leaves him at the moment of his decision to give up his pursuit of the dream of an ageless, always young frontier. In accepting his limitations of one place to make a home for himself and thus in accepting his *place* of limitation, Sycamore has in effect become a member of Azuza society. What is the dramatic result of such a choice, as Shepard presents it? Sycamore becomes an old man physically, but he gains a sense of ease. He no longer fears someone behind his back, he can rest without thought of having to make a "next move." As

Sycamore says in the last lines of the play, he's done his bit, he's lived his life, he's had his yearnings, and now he wants to settle down into a quieter life. In his own words, "There comes a time to let things by. Just let 'em go by. Let the world alone. It'll take care of itself. Just let it be."

Shepard put *The Unseen Hand* at the beginning of his collection and also gave to it the title of his volume. The play itself was not one of his popular successes, nor one that Shepard enthusiasts recognize as a seminal work or a neglected masterpiece. The reason for Shepard's attachment to it must lie elsewhere. In some ways the play represents a Shepard not yet caught in his quandaries, a Shepard beginning on his journeys. He has been able to mix his affection for science fiction, the world of the possible-impossible, with his love for traditional Western values, the world of receding but still redeemable Good and goods. Adolescent in vision, perhaps "embarrassing" to Shepard years after its production, the play shows how he is developing from the narrow world of high-school cheerleading in Duarte, California, to the alien world of oppression in New York slums and its tendrils to the Third World (and whatever Fourth, Fifth, and Sixth Worlds of time and sequential space may come). The Unseen Hand of mind control in this play is overcome by the unseen spirit of American Indian lore and beliefs. (Willie's chants as he transports himself into his mind trances are variants of a "strange ancient language.") Although everything in *The Unseen Hand* has a cartoonlike character, the oversize heroes are safe from the blemishes of reality's compromises and demeaning cuts of legendary proportion. The power of the cartoon, like the Saturday morning cartoons on television screens in Duarte in the 1950s, becomes the power of myth, a blanket of sustenance through the agonizing, doubtful day. Seen in context, *The Unseen Hand* is Shepard's tribute to the cartoon in which the good guy gives a wallop to the bad guy and the hero rides off into the sunset to find his valley of lone splendor.

Shepard experienced a number of disappointments at the end of the 1960s. Although he continued to earn respect from critics, his work also drew barbed criticism, and he suffered from the tension and the peer pressure of his theater world. At the same time he was trying to justify the Rockefeller and Guggenheim Foundation grants awarded him during the past two years by writing a big play, one that would establish him as a playwright aware of social concerns. It was during this period that he composed *Operation Sidewinder*.

Its failure, and the disintegration of his personal life—a tempestuous affair with the rock singer Patti Smith led to a brief separation from his wife in 1970 and to her departure to a separate apartment in Brooklyn—had a traumatic effect on him. Possibly he felt he was repeating his father's pattern of desertion; later, he would admit, in an interview published in 1984, that his excessive drinking was a manifestation of Manichean identity with his father.

First scheduled for production at the Yale Drama School in late 1968/early 1969, *Operation Sidewinder* was withdrawn because of pressure from black student groups angered at Shepard's emblematic portrait of three black revolutionaries. The play was produced a year later at the Vivian Beaumont Theatre in Lincoln Center (March 12, 1970) under the direction of Michael A. Schultz, in what was hoped would be Shepard's introduction to mainstream success. Shepard was a participant in the performance, playing the drums with the Holy Modal Rounders band that was an integral part of the drama. Instead of acclaim, *Operation Sidewinder* became Shepard's first major critical disaster.

The narrative turns of the play are epic in concept, as if Shepard had finally decided to write a "big" play by confronting issues of moral responsibility. A robot, or sidewinder, has wandered off from his scientific reservation. He finds a spot in the vast New Mexico desert where a couple are speaking to each other in endearing terms as if they were on a honeymoon (the woman's name is Honey). Actually they are on their way to Reno for an amicable divorce; they are journeying together because it is cheaper for two people to travel together than for one to go singly. Attracted by the sexy blonde woman, the sidewinder makes a pass at her, embracing her with its snakelike tentacles. At first the woman enjoys the unique embrace, but she becomes alarmed when the robot refuses to relax its grip. Running off for help, her husband Dukie enters a garage where a polite young mechanic is attempting to repair a car, which had been wrecked by an angry Young Man. The Young Man is hyped-up, in need of a fix for himself as well as for his wrecked car; his temper is short. When he sees Dukie running into the garage (it is in the middle of a desert, with no other building in sight), the apparition's arms flailing and a voice screaming for help, the Young Man shoots him. When the nice mechanic chides the Young Man for his criminal act, the Young Man shoots the complainant. (The language of the mechanic will in essence be repeated in *The Tooth of Crime,* when Crow tells Hoss, after Hoss has shot the referee of their fight, that he didn't do the right thing. Both the mechanic and

Crow will say that the killer has *now* overstepped his bounds, that he has crossed a divide he cannot rejoin at will.)

Fleeing the scene, the Young Man finds Honey and the robot, with its tentacles still securely around her waist. The Young Man waits for old Billy, a Western hobo, to show up. He gives Billy money to give to Mickey Free to purchase guns to be used against the American military establishment. Mickey Free is fighting for his people, the besieged American Indians, and needs guns and military hardware. Having got his instructions, Billy wanders off the scene, and the Young Man moves off as well. The Young Man cannot stay still: movement is his constant.

Mickey Free arrives on the scene to find Honey still bound in the robot's arms. He cuts off the head of the robot and stuffs it in his pouch; it is Mickey's symbolic victory over the machine. Mickey then leaves before the Young Man returns. At this point the play becomes a chase comedy. Everyone wants the robot's head because the robot is more valuable in its wholeness than in its parts. Among the chasers are three black revolutionaries who want to stir up political dissidence; scientists who want their experiment (the robot) back; the military who want to use the robot for their programs. Ironically, Mickey Free will also be in search of the robot's missing part (in Mickey's case, the body, since he already possesses the robot's head). Mickey will be told by a seer-witchwoman that the Apocalypse, the Promised Day of a New Era, can only come when the body and the head of a strange robotic phenomenon are joined. The joining will take place in a comic-ironic episode in which the Young Man and Honey will play a major (to their surprise) part. Troopers will storm the Indian reservation and pump bullets into Mickey Free, the Young Man, and Honey; the bullets will have no effect as the three have become ethereal spirits, having gained entrance into the primeval space of the Indian sky.

Shepard's use of intertextual song (some of which he created, some of which he borrowed from Hopi chant and other sources) "alienates" each scene, that is, it obliges the audience to see it as a particular provocation and to react to that provocation of direct or subtextual accusation. The particulars are subsumed in the final scene in one great leap to a mystical truth—the Indian, Mickey Free, and the Young Man and Honey achieve real substance by losing their bodies and floating in the free air of the universe. The American Indian, enslaved by the American military or starved by the American political nexus or corrupted by the temptations of American capitalism, at last transcends his injustices and his colonial overseers. The bullets of the American troopers as they storm into the Indian compound cannot penetrate Mickey Free's body, for he is beyond their reach.

Each "frame" or scene is codified by a song, in the sense of a coda at the end of a musical frame; each song is about some form of imprisonment, whether physical, psychic, or psychological. Shepard in effect is analyzing different people's different ways of confronting isolation from their selves or from their community. One of the imprisonments he dramatizes is the exploitation of American blacks, but Shepard does not applaud the black protest movement of the 1960s. Such a movement to politicalization of all means to freedom, as expressed by his portrait of three black revolutionaries and the young white female carhop who brings them their fast-food order, goes against the grain of his anarchic personal feeling. A political animal in his reverence for the individual's right to hold fast to an apolitical stance, Shepard saw in the black protest movements of the 1960s a politicized drama that repeated the subjugation of personal attitude and behavior in the name of political and societal goals. His portrait of the young white female carhop who pretends a connection of sympathy to the black protest movement is more denigrating than his commentary on black activists. The carhop has no idea of what she is saying, except that she likes the image of herself saying it, whereas the black revolutionaries know what suffering they and their forebears have experienced and do not pretend any obfuscation of their methods. The students at Yale Drama School who protested Shepard's portraits were correct in perceiving that Shepard was criticizing the politicization of the black protest movement; what is unfortunate is that more black students did not see that Shepard's way was an alternative method and not a censure of the subjugated group. Shepard's recourse was to a mysticism of the American Indian, a reward to be gleaned not from achieving rightful political and economic subsidy but from transcending all subsidy of material means. Such an anarchic testament was anathema to the politics and spirit of the decade, not only for political blacks but for the peace movement of post-1968 and the anti–Vietnam War protesters, and it is not surprising that Shepard found himself in exile in his own land. He had always been on the fringe of things. Now he was openly on the outside of the bohemian world, a world to which his inner being belonged. At the same time he was unable to join the world of bourgeois rationalizers, a world whose values he scorned and whose values he believed had betrayed his parents and grandparents.

In *Operation Sidewinder* the distinction between ends and means may be seen most profoundly in Shepard's turn to the science fiction of his robotic sidewinder, and to the variant attitudinal responses Shepard gives to each of the characters vis-à-vis the robot. In the opening scene the robot has wandered out of the laboratory, gone off from the scientific reservation. (The ironic parallel to the Indian reservation, a later setting in the play, is apparent.) The sidewinder is thus characterized immediately as an oddball robot, an eccentric of his species: he does not follow instructions as a robot should. Shepard satirizes the military mind and its rigidity of narrowness in an early scene between a colonel and a captain involved in the scientific research project on the robot. The colonel thinks himself superior to the captain because the colonel breeds dogs and thus is training dynamic animals while the captain has assigned himself to a static machine. Clearly, neither of them has a conception of knowledge higher than their grasp of occupational prominence. The mad scientist, Dr. Vector, does have a mind that grasps at the unknown, but it is tempered only with and by scientific precepts. Dr. Vector becomes ecstatic over the news of the robot's wandering in the desert—he sees in the occasion an opportunity for new depths of knowledge. Yet Shepard makes clear that Vector's research, like his name, is concerned totally with scientific angles. He is all laboratory, all-science (rather than classically omniscient), all-vectors—he has no interest in anything but observation, the root of science. His brilliance is dimmed by the shadow of the scientific scalpel that inhabits his cutting mind. If Dr. Vector is pure science, the other characters are impure humans, motivated by a variety of self-interests. The Young Man (given only an allegorical name to represent one dominant kind of young American of the 1960s–1970s) wants money for drugs; the discovery of the robot means he has a means to his fix. Honey and her husband Dukie are innocent bystanders caught in the crossfire of the seekers after the robot. Honey is the sweet image of a sexy blonde figure of the age, the Marilyn Monroe woman who tries to please her husband even as she is divorcing him.

Honey and Dukie, on their way to a divorce court, are sharing expenses, thus turning an expensive journey into a bargain vacation. Honey's reaction to the sidewinder who wanders into their vacation spot is typical of 1960s consciousness: as a sex symbol she responds to the sidewinder, once he has clamped himself round her, as an opportunity for a new thrill. When the sidewinder refuses to give up its hold on her, Honey realizes the titillation has greater bonds than she anticipated. She sends her husband off for help; he in turn is murdered in a garage that houses at the moment of his plea a paranoid killer. (The couple bear resemblance to the nitwits in *La Turista,* who presumed that they could titillate with a primitive culture and depart from their dance whenever they chose.) Dukie's murderer is the Young Man, who in a fit of rage at encountering difficulties in having his car repaired, shoots the mechanic—Shepard's version of shooting the messenger who brings the bad news.

The Young Man will find Honey and the robot in the desert, but not before Mickey Free, the Indian, has cut off the robot's head and stuffed it into his Indian-beaded pouch. Mickey Free, at this stage of the play, is a divided man—he wants freedom and equality for his people; he has chosen violence and politicization as his means of achieving his goals. He has allied himself with gangsters to establish a source of supply for guns and armored hardware. The corrupting compromise is symbolized in Mickey Free's cutting off the head of the robot—not until the robot is rejoined will a new day dawn for the Indian, and for the converted Young Man and Honey. The joining of the robot's parts will become the announcement of the day of the Apocalypse. For Mickey Free, it will be an explosion into the being of immateriality, a nonbodied being floating in the air above the material world. For the other characters, the joining of the severed robot will lead not to material gain, or military dominance, or political victory, but to the knowledge of defeat of their limited, corrupt goals. The military will gain nothing by its invasion into the Indian hogan where the robot's parts have been joined, for the robot has been consumed in the freeing/joining religious ceremony. Nor will the black revolutionaries gain their goals as a politicized community, since they will not have the robotic means to destruction of enemies of the black man. (The black revolutionaries had attempted to bribe Mickey Free into poisoning the area's water supply by dripping hallucinogenic drugs into a reservoir, but Mickey Free balked at the crime.)

One other character has a relationship to the robot: old Billy, the grizzled Gabby Hayes look-alike traveling man, the desert rat or Western hobo. He is Shepard's familiar image of the traditional values of the Old West. Like those values, Billy appears frayed but will eventually prove a triumphant individual. Billy is first seen with pans tied round his body, a convenient way to provide self-sufficiency on one's travels (the same image device is given to Rabbit in *Angel City,* who is also an acolyte of old Western values). Billy is forgetful, he is lazy, he tends to prefer a good drink to a good or hard thought, but his values have validity beyond their lack of surface appearance. When he is interrogated by the military about the identification of the Young Man, he rightfully says he doesn't know the name of the Young Man. He has been calling him by any number of proper first names: *Danny, Jimmy.* The proper name does not matter, but the allegorical or characterological one does: he is the Young Man, he is Young America in the 1960s. Billy's method is then both one of unconventional wisdom and of self-survival, particularly for someone with a liquorified, addled brain. The rest of the world rejects Billy as a dreamy, sodden fool who lives in his desert of the mind, but Billy, of all the characters in the play, stays the same: he holds his own against the temptations of the new and shiny, and his self-arrest keeps him going strong. Shepard's statement about Billy—that he is out of touch—is to be taken in complete reverse form.

Though Shepard has little in common otherwise with D. H. Lawrence, perhaps the twentieth century's most passionate preacher in English of connectedness, he shares with Lawrence a vision of polarity to end all other and lesser polarities, a joining of body and head, mind and heart, reason and feeling. Shepard finds his vision of unity in the primitiveness of American Indian folklore; such "primitiveness" is a return to primal consciousness that travels beyond the boundaries of rational borders. His science fiction becomes mythic lore, a 1960s blend of fantasized space peace, a universe in which humanity can go home again to a prelapsarian garden, a peace of space in which all can float free from the pressures of human misapprehension. Before the journey to such an end can be achieved, however, a number of pretenses must be shed. These include the rationalized journeys of personal and communal violence; the miscalculations of scientists like Dr. Vector who pervert science into a kind of science-for-science's-sake field of operation, without concern for morality or humanism; the devious demonstration of political revolutionaries; and the mindless passions of adolescent gangsters. Once these illusions are shed, the individual can step into a world touched by inviolate spirits. Apolitical as Shepard may have been (and remains), he identifies himself with several movements and/or consciousness of his youth's age: the pacifism of civil disobedience; the return to nature and native America; the surrender to anarchic mysticism as a higher form of understanding. At the same time he rejects other movements of his decade, movements that by their nature, and whatever their goals of group freedom and equality, mandate a process of politicization of emotion.

Naming, or onomastics, also has its significances in this play. Dr. Vector, Honey, the three black revolutionaries (Blade, Blood, Dude); Dukie, with its John Wayne allusiveness; the occupational names (the Colonel, the Captain, the Sidewinder, the Mechanic, the Forest Ranger) are utilized by Shepard for linkage with earlier and later works as well as with easy identification of satiric object. Shepard also continues to use two of his familiar images: the cricket and the coyote, each a part of desert life, both necessary for survival of the whole being.

5

The Plays: 1970–1974

Although many of his projects from 1968 to 1970 proved abortive, Shepard earned enough money from them and from other productions to buy a farm in Nova Scotia in 1970. A significant royalty came from the inclusion of the third act of *The Rock Garden* in the "erotic revue," *Oh! Calcutta!,* "anthologized" by Kenneth Tynan in 1969. On their farm, Shepard, O-lan, and their son spent the summers away from the demands and pressures that Shepard felt were increasingly impinging on him—demands that became the subject of several of his plays.

In 1971, suffering from personal and career problems, Shepard decided to move into self-exile in England; O-lan and their son joined him. Shepard thought he would get a job as a musician in one of the rock groups he admired there, but although he jammed and played in clubs, he remained foremost a writer. He lived in the unfashionable Shepard's Bush neighborhood and worked with several theater groups. He wrote *The Tooth of Crime, Blue Bitch* (performed on BBC Television in 1973), *Geography of a Horse Dreamer, Little Ocean* (a gentle comedy about pregnancy that was given a production by the Hampstead Theatre Club; Shepard and O-lan had moved to a flat in Belsize Park near Hampton Heath); and *Action.* In an interview with Kenneth Chubb and the editors of *Theatre Quarterly* ("Metaphors, Mad Dogs, and Old Time Cowboys") Shepard said, "It wasn't until I came to England that I found out what it means to be an American."

Shepard's comment may be seen as that of the self-exile who needs distance for a clearer view of his roots. While in England he was able to reflect on his family, still present as a force in his memory but at a safe enough distance from invasion of his present quarters. He was able to admit his appreciation of American values without the anxiety of possibly offending would-be (in Shepard's view) sophisticates critical of American parochialism. His growing strength in seeing American values as liberating rather than constricting, as complex sentences of nurturing ambiguity rather than an alloyed compound of devious sentimentality, enabled him to face his own problems. It was in England that he freed himself of drugs, although he began drinking heavily as a compensation for the drug withdrawal. It was also in England, through the director Peter Brook, that Shepard met and studied with the philosopher, G. I. Gurdjieff. Gurdjieff's system and training had a calming effect on Shepard.

Shepard returned with O-lan and their son to the United States in 1974.

Mad Dog Blues, a "two-act adventure show" with music, was first produced at Theater Genesis in New York (at St. Mark's Church on the Bowery) on March 4, 1971, under the direction of Robert Glaudini; the production was mounted before Shepard's departure for England. It employs a technique common in Shepard's work, that is, the use of two men, somewhat different in temperament and social/personal attitude, but joined by a sense of their brotherhood/kinship. Shepard carries the technique to uncommon depth as he has the two men indulge in their wildest fantasies. The fantasies are mythic in design—that is, the two men journey through past and present eras of both history and racial memory, of both personal desire and social construct. In the dramatic process Shepard's characters have a great deal of fun. They often interrupt the stage action to announce their pleasure or distress; at times they berate the playwright for the difficulties into which he has placed them. In no other play is his admiration for Bertolt Brecht's "alienation" and "epic" stage techniques so apparent as he creates confrontation between character and audience and dares his viewers to doubt the veracity of the illusions he is drawing under their eyes.

The two protagonists are buddies to begin with and friends to end with. One, Kosmo, is the Shepardian hero already known to his fans: slim, tall, full of "heroic pose," all body and little mind, a loner with the strength of the American cowboy in him. The other, Yahoodi, is shorter and darker; he passes himself off as a "nigger." The two bear resemblance to Shepard and Charlie Mingus, Jr., and to their young days as roommates on the Lower East Side. There is a darker side to their portrait as well: one is a self-loathing white, the other a self-hating black. Each needs to come home to himself as a self-loving whole. As the play opens, the two are seen on opposite sides of the stage, separated by a great distance that seemingly they can cross over, but not until the last scene will they have crossed the gulf separating them.

Before the action begins, the prologue tells the audience that the Shepardian character, Kosmo, is like "a leaking brain" who has no control over his temper—he is violent in his reactions to frustration. This Kosmo is a potential danger in his hatred of politics, philosophy, and religion. He asks for God's help in setting the world to rights. Kosmo, then, is a fundamentalist, a mindless one who appears to reject the ideas of the decade that has just passed. Though Kosmo is open enough to admit he is "hoping to find a home" he is a closed mind on most matters.

Yahoodi, his buddy, is described as snakelike or street-smart, a dude who "prefers isolation" but "hates to be lonely." Shepard's portrait of Yahoodi is also one of a lost soul, but one not to be trusted. Yahoodi is a mean critter who, more in control of his violence, is deadlier in his assaults and deceits than Kosmo.

Admitting to his confusion with the world, Kosmo yearns to find a woman like Marlene Dietrich, who will whip him into shape. Irony being an invidious streak in Shepard's view of life, it is not surprising that Kosmo will not get an organizer and a whippersnapper like Marlene but rather a fat and pleasure-loving female, a consuming lover like Mae West. She is the kind of woman who takes men as they are, and after taking them for what they are worth, dropping them.

Kosmo's head is also filled with Jack Kerouac images—he yearns to get on the road and move to a legendary kingdom of Rock music and Beat pleasure. From his side of the stage, Yahoodi is yearning to find a jungle where there are real snakes. He's had his fill of the urban life, he wants an illusionary push into a garden of imagination with real vipers.

Thus Shepard sets the play in motion for the odyssey of the two men—searching for treasure, calling on their fantasies, goading themselves into finishing the "play" they keep unlocked in their mind. What Kosmo and Yahoodi want is not so much a pot of gold as a little rainbow that will wet their dry yearnings into a blissful climax.

Much criticism of *Mad Dog Blues* has centered on Shepard's use of movie lore and legend in the play. Humphrey Bogart, *Treasure of Sierra Madre,* B. Traven, Mae West, Marlene Dietrich, and Gabby Hayes, all come in for satiric exploitation. Shepard also employs other legends—Janis Joplin, the Grateful Dead, Jack Kerouac, Paul Bunyan, Captain Kidd, and the Ghost Girl, among them. His aim is not to puncture the legends but to reveal how they function for his two protagonists. Their appearance on the stage in physical form is a manifestation of the imagination of it that Shepard has spoken of elsewhere. They are more real in Kosmo's head and in Yahoodi's head than they ever were in real life; they are expressions of character that go beyond biographical realism.

Another work presented before Shepard's flight to self-exile in England, and which suggests his nadir of anxiety, is *Back Bog Beast Bait,* a one-act play with music, and first presented at American Place Theatre on April 29, 1971. O-lan Shepard, his wife, was one of the leads; the director was Tony Barsha, once Shepard's rival for O-lan. The play was revived in 1984 at La Mama in New York. Shepard was not satisifed with the production; he pulled it from the double bill with *The Unseen Hand* and substituted *Forensic and the Navigators,* a pairing that gives a greater cohesivenes to the evening, since both *The Unseen Hand* and *Forensic and the Navigators* are indebted to Shepard's intellectual fascination with science fiction. *Back Bog Beast Bait* draws essentially on myth and legend and the fear of the unconscious/subconscious for its tenor and texture. Ostensibly the story of a beast, Tarpin, who wanders the hills in a Western state and who devours children, the three-scene drama is a manifestation of the fear, psychic and mythic, endemic to growing up in mountain and swampland. Tarpin is reputed to have two heads and to snort like a pig. His goal of eating all the children in the swamplands and the mountains behind them—in what Shepard identifies at one point as Arapaho Indian country—is to destroy a civilization by consuming its young. Maria, attempting to protect her son, has hired two gunfighters to slay the beast. Her daughter was killed by the pig-beast at the moment she was growing into a woman (and thus able to reproduce); Maria's husband has been lost ever since he went off in pursuit of the pig-beast.

Into Maria's house come the two gunfighters. One is Slim, the archetypic Shepard hero, slim, Waspish in looks and background (though not of wealthy stock), but this Slim cowboy hero is getting old. He no longer draws his gun so quickly, and he is finding himself lonely out there on the range/desert. He has hired a sidekick, Shadow, a younger version of himself but shorter and darker. In the two figures Shepard is contrasting two generations of gunfighters: Slim still wears cowboy boots and spurs, a Western hat with a braided Indian band round it, and he carries pearl-handled revolvers. Shadow wears mocassins, a flannel shirt and a Sioux headband—he has some of the accoutrements of the hippie about him. Shadow does not have the veneration of the Western code that informs Slim's way of life; he is also more interested in girls and sex than Slim is. Slim can exist with a masturbatory dream, or a helping hand (as he asks of Maria), but emotion, even transient, is beyond him. At one point Slim talks of protecting the ranch and his wife and kids—Shadow correctly deflates Slim's assertions by pointing out that Slim never had a family or a ranch. Shadow compares Slim to a woman in love—presumably the love is for the dream of romance and heroism.

In spite of the threat of the beast looming outside, Shadow goes off into the night to find himself a girl. When he has returned in the next scene, he's slept with Gris-Gris, an Indian girl who may also be a witch, a demon, and/or a swamp beast. What is without question is that she has a foul mouth and is a spitfire.

Shadow may be Shepard's representation of himself knocking down his father's ideals of the West. There are enough clues in the play to suggest that Slim is modeled after Shepard's father—he lives on the desert, he is pictured in long underwear (long underwear in Shepard is a sure clue to the body of his father, both as a means of keeping warm and as a memory of old-style, utilitarian clothing). Slim refuses any drugs but admits to a love of alcohol, the indulgences clarifying one generation's preference for addiction over another. The two gunfighters are in effect father and son rather than brothers under the skin; they represent two parts of a man, two sides of tradition. Slim wants to abdicate his gunfighter role; he's been a gunfighter too long, there are always up-and-coming gunfighters at his back. At one point he lyricizes his feelings, saying he would love to gain back the power to kill, if only for one moment, but he knows his power is gone. Slim cannot feel anymore, he doesn't "feel a thing," his passion and his life are over the hill.

Into the house has come a preacher who has been assaulted by the pig-beast. He is deranged after his mauling, and he speaks in flaming visions of the Apocalypse. Maria tends to him, but even after a good night's sleep, the preacher does not regain his sanity. When Shadow suggests everyone eat a mushroom he has picked the night before with Gris-Gris, Slim cautions against it. He warns that the mushrooms may be poisonous. Shadow eats one anyway and so does the preacher. Each of them goes mad, and Slim accuses Gris-Gris of being an agent of the pig-beast. Slim charges that Gris-Gris persuaded Shadow to pick the mushrooms. Slim threatens to kill Gris-Gris unless she releases Shadow from his spell, but Gris-Gris laughs at Slim and taunts him to try his power on her. Slim realizes he has lost his power and admits his condition of defeat to himself.

All of the characters appear to be giving in to madness at this point. Earlier, at the climactic end of scene 2, Maria had found her son dead in his bed. Now she is lost in a miasma of dark sorrow, endlessly chanting prayers to a shadowy vision. The preacher is talking of the Apocalypse. Shadow is going through convulsions, and Gris-Gris is delirious as she plays demonic music on her fiddle. The beast enters the scene, but no one notices him. He comes downstage, faces the audience, and appears, in Shepard's words, "alone and helpless." He moves offstage, quietly, still unnoticed. But if the beast has been quiet in his tracks, the human characters grow noisily wild. Gris-Gris hoots like an owl, the preacher slides across the floor like an alligator, Shadow snorts and paws like a bull, and Maria screams like a wildcat. Slim tries to resist the pull to hysteria, but he cannot hold out against the demon power. Like Dr. Faustus, he tries to delay his fate. He begs, "I ain't had my day!" He wants more time to get back on his feet and to become a real fighter. He asks not to be taken *now,* to be given "a little bit longer." Slim knows his time is up, however, because he's "beyond prayers now." Yet he asks forgiveness because he "never chose" his moves. Then, having made his apologies, he accepts his fate of transformation into a coyote (or to become the coyote that has always lain fallow in him). He begins howling and yapping. He says, "I am the beast. The beast is me." "Infected with desert life," he accepts his condition as a desert creature shut out from the companionship of other animals.

The many threads Shepard weaves in *Back Bog Beast Bait* can be unraveled. One theme is death, either physical death or the moment when something must be given up, something must move on. Slim, the gunfighter, has outlived his time. Into this familiar concept Shepard invests the image of his father fleeing to the desert as a way out of domesticity. Each of the characters has his own beast within him. The "real" beast, if he exists, is not even noticed when he appears because the subconscious beasts in us take up all the space of imagination. The problem with *Back Bog Beast Bait* is not its content, but its failure of development of ideas and imagery in any consistent shaping of imaginative force. The characters lack vitality because they are given little chance to grow into their roles, except momentarily and abruptly. Slim's pathos at the end, when he accepts the eternity of his coyote identity, has not been prepared for, except as an intellectual conception.

The songs that serve as choral mood—music by this time has become an integral part of Shepardian drama—are the most vital parts of the play. They introduce the first scene and create another mythic resonance to the proceedings. Their presence strengthens the intensity of the drama, keeping its claustrophobic appeal dominant, but the beast in this drama is never realized as frighteningly profound.

Shaved Splits (1970), *Cowboy Mouth* (1971), and *Back Bog Beast Bait* (1971) are Shepard's most savage satires. In these plays, written shortly before his self-exile, he hit out at a host of subjects. The most familiar targets are those who made demands on him—his audience, his backers, his critics. It is as if, having tried to please for so long a time, he is now tired and resentful of the time he has given to his efforts. Certainly the fear of having lost his talent pervades the plays of this period as well as a backlash of anger at those who would expropriate his talent. Whereas, in earlier work, the fight between convention and eccentricity was an amusing battle with a lighthearted victory to the eccentric, the plays in this period involve a battle for man's soul in which no one is spared excoriation. *Mad Dog Blues,* a satire written during this period, escapes Shephard's web of descent into despair, but only at the cost of dissembling his world into a vaudeville carousel. In *Cowboy Mouth,* no such alternative is presented. Indeed, in *Cowboy Mouth,* there are two hells awaiting the play's characters: one lies in killing oneself, the other lies in the death of contemporary life.

A short play in one act with music, and with Patti Smith credited as coauthor, *Cowboy Mouth* was first presented at the Traverse Theatre in Edinburgh on April 12, 1971, under the direction of Gordon Stewart. It received its first American production at the American Place Theatre a few weeks later on April 29, under the direction of Robert Glaudini; Shepard and Patti Smith played the roles based on themselves. The play was paired with Shepard's *Back Bog Beast Bait,* and O-lan Johnson, his estranged wife, was in the cast of this accompanying play.

Cowboy Mouth is Shepard's version of his relationship with Smith and of his life in her tiny Greenwich Village apartment. Abrasive, feisty, flaming in her hairstyle and clothes, Smith proved a fascination for Shepard, unsure of himself and vulnerable at the time. One can see again the swings and conflicts in Shepard: as a middle-class youth sowing his wild oats with a liberated woman, as a writer exploring the boundaries beyond the conventional, and as a genuine artist in search of a divine fix. Smith offered some glimmer of all these prizes.

Cowboy Mouth evolves as well from Shepard's analysis of his—and the artist's—conflicts with bourgeois morality and the loyalties in friendship and family relations. As the play opens, Cavale (the character based on Smith) and Slim (the character Shepard ties to his own identity) are quarreling. Slim wants to go back to his wife, yet he is staying on with Cavale. Cavale taunts him with the soubriquet "Mr. Yesterday" because (she says) Slim cannot move on to a next step; always he is tied to the past and to the values the past has inflicted on him. She tells Slim that he is preventing his own freedom (and spoiling hers) by "placing" things. He has to have a "place"—a label—ready for everything, a variant of the conventional saying, everything in its place. (Shepard is fond of using this technique, whether consciously or instinctively, and his language mimics the cliché at the same time it alludes to its original, unadulterated strength of insight.) Slim thinks at times that the Brooklyn flat with his wife may be his "space," but he will not make the decision to fly there yet. Cavale has other means of flight: drugs, fantasy, ecstasy of vision. She allies herself with the crow-raven she keeps in her apartment. She thinks of the crow as an extension of the French decadent writers Gérard de Nerval and Baudelaire, both of whom used drugs to raise their visions to exalted states of being. Cavale's crow is dead, but she speaks to it as if it were her living "baby." Indeed, Cavale is after a "baby," a creature to whom she can surrender her love. In effect, she is after a means of submission to a religious experience, a conversion to a faith that annihilates doubts and anxieties. She is looking for a savior.

Cavale becomes, then, a perverse pilgrim wanting a Jesus in a rock or a Johnny Ace singer. Slim is a more cautious zealot. He wants out of his role as savior. A few years ago he might have toyed with the performance if it could help those who asked his aid, but he feels spent now. Thus, he is angry at Cavale's kidnap of him for her purposes of evangelization; he feels a prisoner of her dreams. Yet, the germ of wanting to please—a germ that in other Shepard plays exposes corruption in modern society—prods Slim into playing with Cavale at her games. Possibly, too, Slim, unable to break with one world for another but hoping to hold onto both—the world of his wife and the world of Cavale—indulges in such games as subterfuge. The game they play most intensely is the Lobster

Man fantasy. Explicit reference is made to William Butler Yeats's line "What rough beast slouches towards Jerusalem to be born?" (from his poem "The Second Coming") and to the coming apocalypse at the end of the twentieth century: a monster, Cavale and Slim tell each other, will rescue them from living hell. Their first "play" is to telephone the Lobster Man for a take-out order; when he arrives at the apartment and steps out of his shell, Cavale sings a rock song in which is intoned a prayer for a monster-savior. In response, the monster takes on the shape of Elvis Presley and begins a Presley-like sex dance. At this point Slim leaves the stage, presumably to return to the more limited visionary space of his wife's Brooklyn flat. He is rejecting the world of the apocalyptic for the world of daily coping, but he does not depart before giving his gun to the Lobster Man. Slim also leaves his guitar, a gesture of rejection of rock salvation. Left alone on stage with the Lobster Man, Cavale has an epiphany of failure. She refers to de Nerval, who "cried lke a coyote" and who carried a crow and a lobster with him on his walks through Paris, and she admits that de Nerval hanged himself on his birthday. He went out screaming like the coyote whose wails are heard offstage in this play (and in many other plays of Shepard). Cavale admits as well that de Nerval's visions of crow and lobster—as *savior* men—went "on cavale" with his suicide, and that was also how she "found" her name. *Cavale,* Cavale laments, is the Italian word for "escape."

The Lobster Man at this point raises the gun he has been given by Slim, pulls the trigger, but the chamber is empty. Nothing happens, except that the stage turns slowly dark.

Cavale's admission of defeat and the Lobster Man's inability to shoot himself are Shepard's comments on the bleak world of the 1970s drug and rock scene: it is an age lacking in heroism and filled with pathetic flights of daydreaming. The failure of the Lobster Man to shoot himself, and thus usher in a blast of new fervency, something he could give as a superrational gesture of mad faith, is also an allusion to the story of Johnny Ace, told early in the play by Cavale. Johnny was a great rhythm-and-blues singer. He was a myth; he played Russian roulette with his life: he blew his brains out. Johnny Ace's shot, stupid by one frame of reference but divine in Cavale's idealization of it, and the Lobster Man's ineffectual rolling of the gun whose blast might signal a new world, are meant as parallels in the audience's ear.

It does not seem surprising, then, that Shepard disposes of rock as a mystique of salvation in his following work. His newer versions of salvation will be more complex but less ambivalent. The pattern of a climactic work that subsumes the themes, ideas, images, and emotional terrain of works leading up to it is evident in *The Tooth of Crime,* a work that issues from *Mad Dog Blues, Cowboy Mouth,* and *Operation Sidewinder.* One can see in these works a groping by Shepard to understand and then to clarify his material. In the plays that lead up to the work ending one cycle of patterns, one wheel's turns of his imaginative breadth, the endings are less resolute than in the climactic play. It appears that Shepard, who often has stated his adversion to endings, whether in drama, in fiction, or in life, is more willing to come to a resolution of conflicts and issues once he has found his path of illumination. His dramatic vision of a roadway out of the morass is not, however, exclusionary even when he makes a choice of judgment.

Self-exile, as noted earlier, brought Shepard to a state of calmer being. It led to the recapture of his vision of optimism. The journey was not easy, for Shepard found disappointment on several counts. He did not become a rock performing star in England's clubs; he quarreled with several of the directors who mounted his new and older work. Yet Shepard received that most nourishing of all food for a writer—his work was highly respected and noticed, and he was in demand in London's off–West End theaters. The greatest achievement of his exile period is *The Tooth of Crime,* a distillation of many ideas and passions Shepard had been harboring for years. In this play written when he was in self-exile in England and produced first at the Open Space Theatre in London on July 17, 1972—the director was another American exilie, Charles Marowitz, who had left the United States in protest against the Korean War twenty years earlier—Shepard was able to bring together those ruling and unruly obsessions imploding within him. The basic premise is one taken from the old West grafted onto the rock music scene—a duel between the top shot (gunfighter, rock star) and a man who wants to take over that spot. The man on top, the star, has weakened with age: he is showing his innate decency, and he comes from an earlier (Western) tradition that allows for such humanistic options as emotion and projective sympathy. That Hoss, the top man, is no ordinary rock personage is made manifest in one of his early confessions, when he tells the audience and his guitar, "So here's another fantasy / about the way things seem to be to me" (act 1). For a rock star, a man used to hard assertions and the stoned tones of everything in his orbit, the use of "seem to be" instead of the declarative "are" shows a modesty in Hoss's nature that bodes ill in the rock world. Later Hoss will make clearer his own defeat when he says: "We're insulated from what's really happening by our own fame" (act 1).

Hoss knows he is flirting with his own mortality by allowing such a decadence of the rock spirit. He knows that, having been on top and away from the spur of peer competition, he has forgotten how mean his compatriots can, on further push, be. He yearns to be like the Gypsies, who feel no guilt for their lack of human sympathy; he yearns to become again that cool and mean man he once thought he was. Yet Shepard indicates that Hoss was always different from his rock others, always a man with feelings that the other stars in the rock world lack.

The first act of the play is given over to Hoss, to his worries and to his realization that the end is nearing: he knows he can no longer play the game because he has lost heart in it. And yet he is not ready to call finis to the game or to hide behind his throne and its shelter of hangers-on. It is Hoss who starts the duel, sending out word to the challenger Crow that Hoss is ready for him. His entourage—his girl Becky, the disc jockey Galactic Jake, his agent/driver Cheyenne, the astrologer Star-Gazer man—all try to buck him up. They say he, Hoss, is the true "marker," but Hoss cannot indulge in their expectations because he knows he has passed his prime. Like the top gunfighter in the West, he cannot rest because some young punk is looking to topple him the minute he lets down his guard. The references to John Wayne and to drawing fast in gun battles become as important here as in Blue Morphan's speeches in *The Unseen Hand,* because Shepard is alluding again to the mythos of the West and to the demise of that mythos. Yet there is a sense of personal allusion as well—Shepard's personal hero as a teenager was John Wayne (notice how often Shepard uses Wayne's nickname, Duke). Like Hoss, Shepard rose from the ranks. He grew up, as he shows in his plays and in his prose poems in *Hawk Moon* and *Motel Chronicles,* a presumed member of the underclass, associating with the blacks and bohemians in high-school days in Duarte. One of Shepard's fond memories is of beating up rich, socially prejudiced kids in front of a Bob's Big Boy's parking lot who attacked him and his black friends. (The same memory has a different side to it in another character's reaction in *The Unseen Hand*—in that The Kid, who appears on stage beat up by a gang of rich kids, feels an outrage in having been betrayed by the ideals of American high-school dreams in which he has proclaimed himself a member; now, as an outcast, he is terrified of having no allegiance and no supporting group, for he does not believe in himself as a member of any outcast group. That Shepard utilizes the incident to give two different versions of it, almost two polarized versions of a character response to a specified incident, accentuates the significance of the event for him and suggests further that he is writing from some personal experience or some collective memory of it.)

Hoss's compassion as a responsible ruler is out of date in a court filled with scheming usurpers. He tries to talk the old confidence into himself, but when Becky tells him he's been "marked," Hoss knows the prediction wil be validated. He says, ironically, that he must be the Top Gun if the Gypsies are out to get him. For Hoss is now the establishment, the *landed* figure: Hoss has roots in the rock world he has hewn. As a gypsy, Crow has no political, social, or ethnic turf, except that of the wandering caravan. Crow thus has no allegiance to humanity, no ties to a family; he is grooved only for the latest killing of success in the rock world. He is not inhibited by any of the considerations Hoss feels within the realm of feeling and thinking. Crow is all of a piece—poised for the kill and the ascent of the rock mountain—while Hoss, in Crow's eyes, has settled in comfortable compromises; in the process he has become a keeper of things rather than a maker/marker or a rocker. Inevitable in the process, in Crow's eyes, is the slow decay of keeping to being caught in the keeping; once one allows himself to be caught up in the system, one becomes a prisoner, a kept man, of the constraining system.

Hoss expresses his yearning for the anarchic freedom of the gypsy, perhaps a yearning for those days on Second Avenue in New York City when he could play like a cowboy/gypsy. He cannot regain that state—spiritually or physically—for the streets have been taken over by gangs, organized hoodlums. Hoss asks Becky, for example, about the situation in the country—aren't there any farmers, ranchers, cowboys, open spaces left for the freedom-loving man? She replies that the only way to be free is to be in on the game and on top of it. You can't beat the system, you have to join it, she tells him. Hoss is not convinced. He has no heart to go only playing in the game because no reward seems meaningful at the end of the contest; the prize is simply a continuation of what has gone before the contest began. Thus, for Hoss, the future now lies in the past—that is, the future is the memory of a future he once dreamed. And yet Hoss fights on in the games and on the records chart, he keeps believing in a code, because he has to believe in something. He has to follow some ideal. Even after Hoss admits that Crow's cold-bloodedness has become the ideal of an emerging society, he wants to fight one more fight for the old values—he wants to uphold the spirit of humanism. He doubts his strength, however: the virtues for which he is fighting are the weaknesses in his armor. Hoss is thus caught in the impossible dilemma of trying to preserve a civilization and a code he knows is doomed and from whose dying clutches he desires release. Hoss has become a tired fisher king in an Eliotic world.

In the second act of the play, the fight between Crow and Hoss begins. The referee, who in Hoss's words in act 1 is a part of the Keepers System, keeps giving points to Crow. Enraged at the system he has supported—that of the Keepers and a benevolent moderation—Hoss shoots the referee. Now Hoss is truly an outcast: he has become a Gypsy outlaw, a creature cast out from the ring of social convention. The scene in which Hoss and Crow discuss his new status is a forerunner of the sadomasochism that will issue in the family plays to come—the leader and victim are brothers under the same family skin. Crow gloats in his telling of the future for Hoss—Hoss will have to forgo his empathy, he'll have to stop indulging in dreams of a better world, he'll have to control any temptation to perform a kindly act. Feeling his oats as the new leader, Crow demands all of Hoss's turf in exchange for lessons on how Hoss must behave as a Gypsy.

Realizing that he has now lost his honor and a way of life that matters to him, Hoss shoots himself in the mouth. Since Hoss and Crow are mouthers—rock singers, poet-commentators of their time—the choice of place for the gunshot is apt. Before he dies, Hoss tells Crow that Crow can exist only because he has never seen himself objectively, from the "outside." Once Crow allows that virtue of insight, he will be doomed, for he will know how pitiably meager a life he has led.

Hoss's suicide may be considered a heroic act, in its own way as cathartic as Oedipus pulling out his eyes. Hoss goes out a Marker, a man whose actions mark a glory, even if the glory is the acknowledgment of tragic defeat. Yet Crow gives Hoss no tragic dignity, and Shepard does not have any of his characters pay tribute to the achievements of Hoss. Indeed, Crow tells his crew to clean up the place—Crow wants no part of Hoss lying around. Crow also takes for himself, as his girl, Becky; to the victor belong the spoils, and Becky, once Hoss's girl, now joins Crow's camp without complaint or lamentation.

Shepard's rejection of the rock and tinsel world in *Angel City, Geography of a Horse Dreamer, Cowboy Mouth, Melodrama Play,* and in *The Tooth of Crime*'s superb fusion of tragic vision is a rejection of materialist society in pursuit of immediate gratification. Such a society consumes its artists, who are agents for the social gratification, and then discards them when the artistic power grows weak. The society is not merely a capitalist world, or one located in the conference offices of the familiar cigar-smoking mogul, but one inhabited by money grubbers, hangers-on, addicted sports fans, and lonely hyped-up drifters. In rejecting this new show-business world of rock he once sought as salvation, Shepard is declaring a perversion of ideals. He will leave this siren music to return to an earlier memory of the possibility of human triumph—the family with all its quiddities of eccentricity. He will not forsake his music, but the music will be slower-paced, infiltrated with the blues of country-and-western lyrics.

Creative artists fear the loss of their gifts: one morning they may wake up and "it" is not longer there. The indefinite "it" is the mysterious creative power, energy, alchemy that distinguishes an artist from someone lacking the gift of the artist. Shepard treats this theme in many plays during the 1970s. It seems a natural theme for him, for he must have been experiencing tremendous anxiety over his rapid rise to success in the 1960s and his subsequent failures a decade later. He had become the golden-haired boy of off-off-Broadway before he was twenty-one years old. Play after play flowed from his imagination and from the lines he had written onto the notepads he carried with him everywhere in his shirt pocket. No self-consciousness stymied him in the first few years of his career, and then a string of failures, a series of missteps, shook his confidence. Shepard deals with the consequences of these attacks on his spirit as early as *Melodrama Play* (1967). Another of his plays on the same thread of consciousness, and often with similar imagery, is *Geography of a Horse Dreamer,* first produced in London at Theatre Upstairs in The Royal Court Theatre, on February 21, 1974; Bob Hoskins, who later became a major British/American film and stage star was in the cast. The first New York production was directed by Jacques Levy at the Manhattan Theatre Club on December 4, 1975.

Shepard calls *Geography of a Horse Dreamer* a "Mystery in Two Acts." The subtitle reference may be to the genre of mystery, a form Shepard mimics in the play, though he more markedly satirizes the

Western adventure genre. The use of characters like the Doctor, described in images reminiscent of one decade's feared fat man, Sydney Greenstreet, suggest that Shepard had the movies in his mind, and particularly the Humphrey Bogart movies of the decade in which Greenstreet, Peter Lorre, and Mary Astor appeared. Such films were a staple of Shepard's teenage days. Shepard may also be using Mystery Play as an allusion to earlier times, that is, as a reference to the medieval drama in which a biblical story was reenacted and a revelation was illuminated for the audience. Certainly the opening image of the protagonist outstretched on a bed, cuffed to its posts, like Jesus on the Cross, signifies an association with spiritual concerns.

The style of *Geography of a Horse Dreamer* sets it somewhat apart from Shepard's other plays in that its language is almost all shorn, clipped prose. Even the descriptions of the hero's dreams are terse and plain. In self-exile at the time he wrote the play, Shepard's language may reflect an inability to get back home to the free-flowing river of his native tongue, or to a loss of his hyperbolic confidence of an earlier decade. It may also reflect the style of the 1940s and 1950s movies he is mimicking: the tough-guy Bogart heroes and the sinister Peter Lorre and Sydney Greenstreet villains. In those films language was short and unsweet; its humor was maniacal but neat. The violence, when it occurred, was quick and to the point; there was no delight in inflicting pain. Pleasure was exhibited in the control of a situation, rather than in violent exploitation of it.

Shepard gives a title to each of the two acts in this play. The first act is called "The Slump," and is given over to Cody's slump in dreaming up winners of horse races. Shepard gives Buffalo Bill's soubriquet, Cody, to his protagonist, and dresses him in cowboy boots, shirts, and jeans; the association is with the Buffalo Bill who descended into selling himself as a circus item. Cody's feet and hands are iron-cuffed to the bedposts. He is blindfolded in order that he not know where he is. Standing guard over him are Santee and Beaujo, agents of Cody's manager, Fingers.

Cody had once been king of the horse dreamers. He had the touch to dream up winners of horse races. Once he had also been a singer and made a hit record, but when his gift of dreaming horse winners was discovered by managers, he was kidnapped by gangsters, set up in a room and made to reveal his visions. Cody had wanted none of it, not even the good days when the hotel rooms and service were munificent, when he could order anything he wanted, when he was "wined and dined." Now he is reduced to a dingy, third-rate hotel in the hinterlands because he hasn't been able to come up with a winner in months.

When did Cody lose the gift? It is suggested early in the first act that his gift started eroding when Cody began to listen to the record on which he sang his hit song. The record in turn induced Cody's yearning for the Great Plains of Wyoming, from which he came and from which his values and inspiration derive. In sum, when Cody realized he had lost his *place,* he began to lose his gift of picking winners; he knew at that point that he was a victim of managerial exploitation. The managers, however, who were exploiting his talents refused to let him drop out of the system. When he attempted escape, they tracked him down and brought him in tow for another performance. Yet, each performance has become more dismal than the last one, and at the present time Cody is unable to "create"—that is, dream up the winners of horse races.

Santee, one of Cody's guards, referes to Cody mockingly as "Mr. Artistic Cowboy." Santee doesn't have much respect for artistic matters, he wants results; Santee is also a dreamless sleeper, one who utilizes sleep for what it is worth and is never bothered by the kinds of things that go on in Cody's mind. The other guard, Beaujo, is more compassionate: he realizes that Cody is a special prisoner in need of special treatment. Beaujo convinces Santee to let Cody get up from the bed on which he is shackled, but Cody has first to promise not to try to escape, as he has tried once before. The sense of a dog or slave, a trapped creature, being allowed a moment's release, is profoundly touching in this scene, as it will be in *A Lie of the Mind,* when Beth's brother allows the errant husband Jake to walk in front of him like a dog and to do tricks on demand for the brother's family.

As he walks around the room, in a half-stupor, Cody tells his guards that he needs space, inner space, and that unless he is allowed it, his situation will decay further. Santee turns angry at what he considers Cody's whimpering and artistic whining—he puts him back in bed with iron cuffs on his arms and legs. From his bed Cody tells the other jailer, Beaujo, that his dreams worked when they came from instinct and not from others' demands.

Cody's "business" of dreaming thus runs at the exact reverse of the normal business cycle: for Cody, supply cannot come from demand, it must come from a source irrelevant to economic need. Cody wails that if he can only listen to his record, to his song of the Great Plains of Wyoming, he will gather the strength to return to his prime energy, but even as he asks, Cody knows Santee will refuse his plea. Santee will have no favored treatment for the "artistic cowboy."

The guards decide to phone their boss, Fingers, because Cody's condition is deteriorating. Fingers tells them to give Cody one last chance; he instructs them to turn Cody over to picking the winners of dog races, a demotion and loss of status but still a part of the system. (Shepard wrote *Geography of a Horse Dreamer* while he was living in England and had become charmed by two British institutions: the pub and the dog-racing track.) Cody falls into a dream-trance and wakes up to announce the winner of a dog race: Black Banjo (close in sound to Beaujo, Cody's compassionate jailer; the device is likely Shepard's tribute to the kind of man caught in a system to which he is innately superior). Cody continues his rambling after he has picked his winner—he hallucinates about the training and discipline of dogs. Most likely the whipping up of words about discipline and winning the race, achieving the prize, is a projection of Shepard's youthful experiences, when his father drove into him the glory of such an approach to life's moments. At one point, the guard Santee employs a threat to use the "rod" on Cody, another allusion to the kind of parental treatment Shepard experienced.

In act 2, "The Hump," the setting announces that times have changed for the better: a fancy hotel room (though not the most luxurious) and clean furnishings. Clearly Cody is bringing in money again. He is picking winners, he is doing his job for the managers, but Cody is still a prisoner, though in a more gilded cage. He is hallucinating about dog training and breeding, and Santee and Beaujo now express their anxiety that Cody be farmed out permanently, let out of the system before a dead workhorse is left on their hands. They have made known their feelings to Fingers, who arrives in the hotel room with a companion, the Doctor. When Cody sees Fingers, the man who has been his exploiter/manager, he cowers and runs to a corner to hide. Feeling compassion for the haggard victim, Fingers tells Cody that he will be set free even though he is still on a winning streak in the dog races.

The Doctor who has accompanied Fingers has been largely silent until this point. Earlier, when he had entered the room, he had turned on the television set, and Fingers had snapped it off. Seemingly the master of the situation, seemingly in control of activities in this room and thus, by extension, the world of his wider commerce, Fingers had told the Doctor, "We're having a conversation," though the conversation was a monologue by Fingers. In that monologue Fingers had revealed how he had found Cody in a Western town. There was no name to the town, but it was a magical place, like no other place on earth. It was vast, lonely, a great ocean of prairie. Fingers felt awed in its presence, he felt God beside him, he felt he was being embraced in the arms of the universe, he felt like a man in the act of prayer. Yet he tells Santee, Beaujo, and the Doctor that he never tried to locate the name of the town. All he knows, and needs to know, is that it exists on the Great Plains of Wyoming.

Now, as Fingers announces his act of compassion—the setting free of Cody—the Doctor, who has been watching a blank television screen, stands up and viciously knocks Fingers down. Fingers begins to whimper, as Cody had done earlier, before the man he acknowledges as his master demon; he chooses obeisance as his recourse of behavior. The scene may be read as Shepard's dramatization of the triumph of mechanization (the Doctor and his TV) over Fingers (the man who still believes in human talk and conversation), and as the defeat of the effete Fingers (he is thin and elegantly dressed and speaks in a mannered unctuousness) by the gross, Sydney Greenstreet–like Doctor, the emperor of hulking fat. Allied with the Doctor is Santee, a simpleminded greedy passenger in life, yet the Doctor passes over Santee to pick Beaujo as his assistant in an operation to be performed on Cody. The Doctor comments that although Santee is a member of the fold of worn-out integrity, Beaujo still has sparks of honor smoldering in him. Therefore Beaujo is to be taken in hand before he otherwise becomes unavailable.

The Doctor explains his operation on Cody while the frightened Fingers continues to whimper in his corner and the innocent, exploited Cody sits numb in fear. In the bone of every dreamer's neck is the place where the gift of dreams resides. When a dreamer's powers start showing signs of slippage, and the dreamer can no longer be taken for granted as a winner, the operation must take place. For in the neckbone of every great dreamer is the source of dream power, and the bone must be removed from the decaying dreamer's body before all its gift of vision is gone. The knowledge of when to operate on a dreamer—of when to decide the dreamer is of no use anymore but may provide the sacrifice of his bone for the exploiter/manager's power—is crucial. If the operation takes place too late, the bone will prove useless.

The Doctor also explains that with enough of the dreamer bones, the power of dream-vision can be secured again. The totality of the bones becomes the Holy Grail, the power of resurrection or of dream command and vision. The Doctor already has collected several dreamers' bones; he has the bag of bones with him. Now it is time for Cody to have his neckbone removed, and to give his gift to the Doctor.

As the Doctor makes the incision into Cody's neck and blood bursts from it, two men break down the hotel room door and enter the scene. They are dressed in Western gear, they are Cody's brothers in spirit and in fact. Their guns blaze across the room, killing the Doctor, Santee, and Beaujo. They take their bleeding brother Cody with them, back home to the Great Plains of Wyoming, where he will regain his spirit, his wholeness.

When they leave, only Fingers remains on stage. A waiter comes in to take Fingers's order (the waiter had been summoned in the first minute of the act). Fingers tells the waiter to put on Cody's record. The song turns out to be a Western country/Mexican ballad, a lyric celebrating the virtues of the old West and of Mexican home.

What is not clear is whether the bone was removed from Cody's neck before the brothers came in to rescue him. The brothers take Cody back to the wholeness of Wyoming, to the West where a mythos is still available for social and personal health, but do they take back a Cody without the dreamer's bone in his neck, or one with a cut neck but the bone still in it? The answer is important, for it would shed light on how Shepard felt at that time toward his blessing/curse, the artist's gift. It might reveal whether Shepard's ambivalence to his gifts, and his desire to flee from them into the comfortable anonymity of the Western mythos and family, was operating then in a yearning for surcease from his talent. The answer would not change the eternal question, one every artist and Shepard among them, has to come to terms with: how to live with a gift that is beyond reason, how to manage the magnificent beast of the artist in a social arena. It would, however, give direction to what may be Shepard's thoughts on the sufferings of the artist in contemporary times. It might provide a clue to the following: is the exploitation of the artist's talents so pervasive in the American system, and subsequently so invidious in the artist's spirit-body, that the only way out for the contemporary artist, once he has entered the world of public attention/performance, is a lobotomy of his dreams? If the answer is affirmative, then Shepard's five-year silence in writing can be understood as his method of retreat from an overwhelming agony.

Action, written in London but first produced a year later in New York at the American Place Theatre on April 15, 1975, is one of Shepard's least-performed plays. Like *4-H Club,* it is an intellectually realized drama, and contains as well, without self-consciousness or mocking irony, references to literature and philosophy, among them Tolstoy, Whitman, and Abraham Lincoln. This latter feature is rare in Shepard's work, for Shepard makes a point of mocking anything resembling an intellectual stance. *Action* is also another of his plays that deals with the question of identity, which in Shepard's work usually takes the form of a struggle between the conflicting forces of desire to hold onto one's familar possessions and/or feelings and desire to go beyond them. The play takes as its premise two men and two women in their late twenties or early thirties, sitting down to a turkey dinner. It is not Thanksgiving, but the dinner suggests a special occasion for which the two women have been preparing for days. Lupe and Lisa wear 1940s' costumes, while the two men, Jeep and Shooter, are dressed in long coats, jeans, flannel shirts, and heavy boots; their heads are shaved.

The four characters represent aspects of character rather than portraits of individually drawn character. *Action* differs from other Shepard work in that Shepard purposefully avoids the convenience of conventional narrative in his drive to the action of individual, momentary confrontations. At first the two men seem like a prism of brotherhood, differing in temperament and vision but related in mystique and gender solidarity. A careful reading of the play suggests that Shepard is not exploring brotherhood so much as, again, the milieu of father and son. Shooter, the elder or seeming elder of the two, has the characteristics Shepard, in the past, has given to characters he teases as a suggestion of his father image. Shooter, as his name implies, is a man of the old West; he shoots straight, he doesn't go in for sophisticated shenanigans; he likes being alone. Jeep, the other male, is more modern (notice the automobile association, as a distinction from the six shooter), more neurotic. It is true that Jeep talks about his fantasy of being Walt Whitman, and of Whitman talking with President Lincoln, but this association is Shepard-Jeep's tribute to the acknowledged virtues of the father and to the standards of bygone years.

Shooter prefers to be alone, but he is aware he has to perform his social duties on occasion. He says, "You have to find out what's expected of you. You act yourself out." The wording is important, for Shooter never is able to be natural: he is always a performer the minute another person enters his space/stage. Even as he thinks he is safe inside his skin, he knows he has to "hunt for the way of being with everyone."

Jeep, by contrast, is explosive. He breaks things when his temper explodes. He smashes several chairs in the apartment during the course of the dinner in the play. His violence does not mask a desire for fraternity: rather, it reveals it as Jeep makes his references to the worlds of peace and understanding of Whitman and Lincoln, Tolstoy and the Russian land beneath him, the ending of the American Civil War. Jeep wants a joining of his disparate parts; in effect, he breaks chairs so that he can find something that will not break in his passage through the apartment. It is Jeep who keeps talking about his fears, and about how he was never allowed to make his choices when he lived in "houses." As Jeep says, "I lived in different houses. I had no choice. I couldn't even choose the wallpaper." Jeep's memorialized allusion suggests Shepard's own wanderings as the family moved around the country before settling in Duarte.

Jeep, for example, refers to an experience of having to wash in the upstairs bathroom and of his fear of the water in the basin/tub. Shooter asks him why he, Jeep, did not tell him, Shooter, of the phobia; Shooter says he would have comforted Jeep. Jeep then describes other painful incidents in his growing up—he refers to experiences in his 4-H Club and Little League baseball activities. Not until he "got arrested," Jeep says, did he know who he was, not until he "got arrested," did he know his "true position." Jeep says that the night he spent in jail, in the confines of the four walls he could not talk his way out of, made him face himself—before that real nightmare Jeep had no idea of "what the world was," and he had "no references" for what took place within him and outside of him that night.

Jeep's concluding monologue recalls Shooter's speech on the four walls he, Shooter, always finds around him, and on Jeep's earlier speech on not being able to leap out of his walls. (Jeep had said the walls were closing in on him, and that any leap he made to flee them would only bring him closer to them. The imagery recalls Shepard's penchant for identification with Icarus, and the happy, proud leap doomed to fall.) The talk of the men—father and son, older and younger man—is centered on flight, but it is also centered on wanting to be caught, on discovering how to join in the family circle in order to be a part of it. Shooter has the most graphic speech on the subject: he tells the story of three moths trying to understand the workings of a candle and its flame. Only the third moth attains true understanding because the third moth joins the flame, flies right into its burning wholeness.

The women are also searching for some kind of understanding, but their search is rooted in more mundane matters. Lupe and Liza are constantly talking about the dinner and the menu for the dinner: what is the *whole* meal to consist of? Lupe is constantly reading a book, constantly trying to discover the "right" place in the book. *Trying to find the right place* is indeed one of the central subjects of the play.

The absurdities of the activities in *Action*—cooking the turkey over an open fire in an apartment (because the turkey "tastes better that way"), hanging out laundry on an open clothesline in the same apartment, smashing chairs easily and finding a dead fish in a bucket of water—are expressionisms of Shepard to convey his theme. All the characters are searching for the right position in which to locate themselves. Jeep's final speech, however, suggests that the four will not discover the desired position in their dinner meeting. Their "references for this" are just not ample enough to change the menu of their future.

Shepard had been a toiler in Hollywood on several occasions, and by 1976 he had massed several years of insight and agony in his travels through tinsel cities of the world. He had no illusions about the resident factories of illusion in which he worked, yet he had harbored one for a long time; he was disabused of this saving grace (for him) after he came into the studio system for the first time. Shepard thought he could remain aloof from the workings of the movie industry while working in the industry he scorned. In his only Hollywood play—that is, his one play devoted to the milieu of the movie city—he addresses this issue, and characteristically he scores himself for his hubris in thinking he could remain above the fray of the dung heap. This concept of invidious corruption, of time as an eroder of integrity, animates Shepard's Hollywood play, *Angel City*.

In the "two-act play with music," first produced at Magic Theatre in San Francisco on July 2, 1976, with Shepard as the director, the hero/protagonist Rabbit is asked to pull a magic trick out of his metaphoric hat for the screenplay of a planned disaster film. He arrives in Hollywood on a horse and wagon. The detail is probably tied, as previously noted, to Shepard's well-known refusal to fly, and thus to the necessity of his taking a long time to arrive anywhere. The reference also ties Rabbit to old forms, old methods of transportation, and, by extension, of traditional values. Literally tied to Rabbit are bundles and sticks and rags of magic Indian potions: these represent the wisdom of the Indian world.

Rabbit has been called in by Lanx and Wheeler to produce another catastrophe movie, a really successful one that will outdo all earlier catastrophe movies, and bring in millions and millions of dollars for the silver screen coffers. Second in command at the studio, Lanx is brass, offensive, and vulgar. His superior, Wheeler (Wheeler and dealer), at first appears the gentlemen of the duo, all politeness and even possibly sensitivity, but he is soon exposed and defiled as any other Hollywood producer. For Shepard, these men are producers of slow poison, their magic entertainment corroding men's insides. Rabbit says that the "products" of such men are "interrupting" his campfires and making him "daydream at night." They are "replacing religion, politics, art, conversation" in modern American society. They are the greatest threat to American society, for they bore from within the human spirit. Rabbit asks himself if he can stay "immune" from the corruption, if he can keep his "distance from a machine like that."

Shepard's play will show that Rabbit is not strong enough to withstand the corruption of a society, and its members, by manufactured dreams. Like Wheeler, Rabbit's skin will turn green. He will grow fangs, and he will become immensely wealthy as he turns into nothing but the illusions of himself projected upon a screen.

The plot of the narrative is almost a staple of what may be called a Hollywood genre: a man of integrity, a person with "old" values and sense of tradition, arrives in the City of Angels. He is offered a great reward if he brings off the greatest disaster movie in history. Rabbit resists at first, for he doesn't want any part of the planned hyperbole. The studio chief Lanx warns that he, Rabbit, thinks he can be like all the others before him—he thinks he can make big bucks for a few weeks, take his money, and run back to the ranch. Not so, says Lanx, echoing Shepard's insight, but from a different perspective: Lanx is doomed, and he wants other souls to join him in damnation.

Rabbit is introduced to Tympani, also a man who came to Hollywood filled with integrity and a belief he could withstand temptation in the form of slow compromise with ideals. Tympani plays the drums and has been assigned to create the right—that is, the adulterated—music for a disaster movie. He arrived in Hollywood with his sense of music as a medium for the soul, but time has imprisoned Tympani within its moving/movie coils. He is a captive soul, someone hired to do a job who cannot go back to the places of his innocence, and who, resisting corruption, cannot surrender to it.

Two doomed souls, Rabbit and Tympani discuss their possible routes of escape, each exposing the self-deceits of the other, each caught in Shepard's view of the web of Hollywood hell. By the end of the play Rabbit will replace Wheeler as the head of the studio; his skin will grow a green slime that makes him dance eternally in an attempt to flee from its punishing sting.

Another major character in the play is Miss Scoons, a role played in the original production by Shepard's wife, O-lan Johnson. Miss Scoons is secretary to Lanx and Wheeler. Her life is absorbed in movies; movies are more real to her in the way they touch her, *reach* her, than any material object or living person. She has a hankering to write a screenplay, act in a film, do anything that will get her more involved every minute with the industry that sustains her illusions. When Tympani plays a drumbeat that, unknowing to him is Miss Scoons's magic connection, she begins to act out her illusions. She transforms herself into a nun, happily washing the studio floors for the glory of God (and Mammon), but her new role is no less an act of self-deception, and self-denigration, than her former ones. At the end of *Angel City* Miss Scoons and Lanx return to their teenage days when the movies first and really caught them. They are willing to sacrifice All for the treat of seeing again a movie that will screen out diversions of reality.

Angel City is a more accessible play than many of Shepard's earlier ones, and its characters are developed in a recognizable way. Shepard, in a foreword, wrote that the viewer should see his characters not as whole people but as a "fractured whole with bits and pieces of characters flying off the central theme." Yet in this play Shepard need not apologize (if ever he needs to apologize for his unique vision) for any dismaying absurdity: Rabbit, Lanx, Wheeler, Miss Scoons, Tympani act out their fantasies in a way familiar enough in theater technique. They are presented expressionistically—Rabbit holding on to his Western rabbit charm piece, Wheeler turning into the devil he has always been under his veneer of an enlightened leader of the movie industry, Miss Scoons trying desperately to get in touch with the illusions that are her real being. These expressionisms draw their power from Shepard's control of his craft: every detail in the play is geared to the theme of Shepard's irony in presenting a world that thinks it creates illusion but relies on the illusions long ago created in myth and collective fantasy.

What the movies do is to exploit illusion, not create it; the people create the illusions and then send word to the movies to reproduce them in variant guises.

One force seems resistant to the corruption of the movies, and to the corruption of myth. That is music, and Shepard gives explicit instructions at the beginning of the play that the saxophonist, who appears in the play as a character, should remain aloof from the other characters. The saxophonist's music is played when there is further revelation of hypocrisy of corruption; the music of the saxophonist heralds the same old changings of corrupt disguise. Yet not all music is resistant to the green slime that will cover the stage at the end of the play. Tympani, the drummer, has sold out, and he, too, like Miss Scoons, will live out a fantasy (his is to be the happy owner of a diner and work as a short-order cook.)

The apocalyptic ending in *Angel City* is the result of Wheeler's anger. Rabbit has dismissed him from his post and taken it for himself; the proclamation of his new position lies in the fangs, long pointed black fingernails, and green skin that constitute Rabbit's physical form. Wheeler seeks not so much revenge as entry into some other world, perhaps a bigger world than the one he last inhabited. Now a nonentity, he walks to the bundles that Rabbit brought with him when the play began. Although Rabbit tells Wheeler that the bundle he, Wheeler, is determined to open will destroy the world—it contains a magic Indian potion—Wheeler refuses to divert himself from his self-appointed task. The bundle promises him a pathway to a perverse grail. When Wheeler asks Rabbit, "What if it's worse than we can imagine?" Rabbit tells him such an occurrence is an impossibility. For the imagination, as Rabbit and Tympani have said earlier, is the most powerful thing in the world. There is nothing greater than the imagination, the two artists Tympani and Rabbit conclude in a round of strophe and antistrophe.

Fear itself, or what Wheeler expresses as his fear, is only the imagination of dying. Such a view seems another aspect of the play's profound theme, for Shepard is talking about the artist and the fear of his talent's dying, a fear more frightening than the death itself. Only the artist has the temerity, and the strength and foolish courage, to approach and unmask the imagination, and therefore only the artist knows the enormity of his act, of his fearsome deed. The movies, in constrast, and those who make them without imagination, rely on familiar illusions; they repeat the safety of custom. Perversely, the movies need novelty, which is dependent on the artist's imagination. Without novelty there is no likelihood of a movie audience; the trade-off is that the artist's imagination is a dangerous thing unless checked by movie programmers. No disaster movies worthy of their tempest can occur, for example, without the artist and his/her imagination; no artist can contain his imagination into a disaster movie unless he adulterates the threads of his imaginative fabric. Either way—manipulation of or surrender to the artist's imagination—the artist finds himself in an awesome adventure with fear. When he pulls back from that fear of confrontation with life's dying into the safety of custom and past practice, he corrupts his being. He becomes the reality of his image of decadence.

6

The Plays: 1975–1985

When Shepard returned to the United States, he went with O-lan to their Nova Scotia farm and began work on his "family plays." He moved to California shortly after, but the economic situation proved difficult. Shepard and O-lan, and their son, were obliged to move into O-lan's mother's house in Corte Madeira, and Shepard took on construction jobs to earn money. His play, *Man Fly,* was turned down in England, but Wynn Handman accepted *Action* for production at the American Place Theatre, and Shepard wrote the short-scene play *Killer's Head* (in which Richard Gere spoke the play-length monologue of a man awaiting execution in the electric chair). More important for his career and his sense of self-awakening was his association with John Lion and the Magic Theatre in San Francisco. Shepard received a Rockefeller grant to work with the Magic Theatre, and one of his first acts was to mount his own production there of *Action* and *Killer's Head.* With his finances improving, he and O-lan moved to Marin County to a ranch. O-lan's mother and her husband Johnny Dark joined them. He began riding in rodeos, a feat he has continued to this day.

Shepard had just moved into his ranch when another of his idols, Bob Dylan, phoned to invite him to join his cross-country Rolling Thunder tour. Shepard's job would be to write a script for the film of the tour—a movie of carnival life in America to parallel the immortalization of carnival life in France in Marcel Carné's film *Les enfants du Paradis.* Though the project proved abortive, and Shepard felt neglected and out of place with members of the show (he left the company for several months, only joining them again for the farewell event at New York's Madison Square Garden), he kept a journal of the experience. That journal was published in book form as *Rolling Thunder Logbook* by Viking Press in 1977.

By 1976 Shepard was back in San Francisco and directing a production of his play, *Angel City,* for the Magic Theatre. He also was to begin his career as a movie star. His brief moment in the Dylan film that was released to poor critical notices and financial returns as *Renaldo and Clara* (1977) caught the eye of the director Terrence Malick, who cast Shepard as one of the male leads in Malick's film *Days of Heaven*. Shepard's film stock soared, and he was offered leading roles in several projects. Selective about his choices, Shepard has remained consistently wary of movie celebrity. Among his best-known roles are the homicidal fanatic in *Resurrection* with Ellen Burstyn; the reporter who befriends Frances Farmer in *Frances;* the veterinarian who teaches the virtues of small-town Vermont life to a big-city girl, Diane Keaton, in *Baby Boom;* and as Chuck Yeager in *The Right Stuff*. As a result of the latter role, he became known in the movie trade as the Gary Cooper of the eighties.

During this period Shepard spent a great deal of his time in the place he now knew he belonged: the theater (but specifically not the Broadway theater world). In John Lion's Magic Theatre in San Francisco, he worked with various directors—one of them became closely associated with him, Robert Woodruff—and with actors in the troupe to create a sense of repertory company and an improvisatory group. His period of self-exile, and his study with Gurdijieff in England, had taught him of his need for team participation, and not merely as a playwright. With the Magic Theater as a support group, he became one of its chief directors, playwrights, and actors. Shepard's interest in directing his own plays also stemmed from his dissatisfaction with the way certain directors in England and the US had interpreted, and in Shepard's view, violated his work.

Shepard was able to effect many of his plans because of a fifteen-thousand-dollar Rockefeller Foundation grant. One of the productions made possible by the grant was *Inacoma,* a venture largely based on improvisatory techniques and theory. Shepard brought the idea of a girl in a coma (the Karen Ann Quinlan news story had given him the idea as a departure point). He instructed the Magic Theatre crew of actors in voice/improvisatory techniques and assigned them such generic roles as the Doctor, the Mother, the Lawyer, etc. He then worked with them in creating a collage of views. He also called for an improvisatory musical background of some twelve or thirteen songs, to be composed in jazz and rock rhythms. The basic premise he gave was that in the first act the Karen Ann Quinlan–like character awake full of life and joy, looking forward to the new day; at some point she would lose her balance, fall, and go into an irreversible coma. The second act is devoted to those who care for her personally and professionally, and the effect of the coma on them.

When the production opened on March 18, 1977, in a third-floor loft in the Fort Mason section of San Francisco, it was called a "work in progress." William Kleb, in "Sam Shepard's *Inacoma* at the Magic Theatre," in *Theater,* wrote that the idea was commendable but that it represented more process than finished product, particularly as it lacked Shepard's language and imagery. The project ended for all intents in its first outing, for the script has never been published, and the production has not been repeated. Yet if *Inacoma* did not prove a triumph, it gave Shepard a chance to revitalize his concerns with improvisatory techniques and to work in a community atmosphere that would nurture his unique talents.

One of Shepard's works that was not performed at the Magic Theatre was one of his most inventive. *Suicide in B♭: A Mysterious Overture* was produced at Yale Repertory Theatre in New Haven on October 15, 1976. Three years later, it appeared in New York at the Impossible Ragtime Theatre. It marks the end of a cycle in which the detritus of Shepard's young manhood is admitted and transcended. After this play Shepard will turn more directly to his family's abiding values for dramatic material. Although his family and his growing up and his youthful experiences have always constituted the material of his plays, they were coded into fantasized fragments. With *Suicide in B♭* out of the way, Shepard will start a fresh look at family matters.

Shepard announces his intentions in *Suicide* in the first line, when the detective Pablo says he is trying to "reconstruct the imagination of it." Two lines later Pablo will continue, "how we suppose it might have been."

In *Angel City,* the play immediately preceding *Suicide in B♭,* the protagonist declares that the imagination is the most frightening of all phenomena because, unlike conventional order, imagination cannot be controlled once given its stimulus. Because he is the most imaginative member of his society, the artist becomes as well its most vulnerable target and potential victim. The artist rightly fears punitive castration because, in exposing society's failures, he is taunting and provoking its ruling members; his artistic duty is not to please but to disturb into thought and wonder. Some societies celebrate the artist and his rightful disturbances, but some turn on such an artist when he is at his weakest point, when he most doubts himself. Shepard was at this low point in the early 1970s when several of his plays were rejected by critics and audiences as incomprehensible, immature, and/or incomplete, lacking in resolution and ending. One solution to the artist's problem is to kill the artist in oneself before society kills him in any of its punitive ways: rejection, starvation, neglect, harassment, or public stoning, among them. When the anxiety is too great to bear, the artist sometimes chooses that option of suicide in any of its variant guises. As Niles says in *Suicide in B♭*, he doesn't mind hanging, but he does fear the slow death of prison life—in the artist's terms, a milieu or environment in which he cannot work at his creations.

Suicide in B♭ then is still another Shepard play about writing a play, or, more accurately, a play about a writer's problems. It is Shepard's most witty play in many respects, owing some of its bubbly airs and elegant ways to the ambience of sophisticated British comedy (an ambience and style Shepard avoided before and after this work). It employs two men as foils for each other, two men who seem on the surface to be brother detectives, but who, again, are partial representations of Shepard and his father, and of their differing attitudes to work and life. The father figure appears in Louis, the detective who had to work his way through night school because the war interrupted his education. Louis identifies himself as a man who loved Tommy Dorsey, the Mills Brothers, Benny Goodman, and the Swing Era. He's a Republican and proud of it; he's proud of having served in the "Real War" (World War II). He has a shrapnel wound to prove his valor. All this biographical data given to Louis is taken from the experiences of Shepard's father.

Shepard himself may be seen more in the protagonist Niles (the one who arranges his suicide) than in the second detective, Pablo. Niles remembers singing in the jungle in Guam; he talks about his mother tying down the bedsheets on the clotheslines in order that Japanese soldiers would not steal them. Niles remembers his mother's pistol on the night table, ready for use in case a Japanese sniper invaded their quarters.

Shepard's fondness for throwing out clues to autobiography is endemic to his work. Since each play he writes (or has written so far) is about himself, his growing up, or his becoming aware of others, he must draw on his experiences. His name tagging becomes his tribute to what he has borrowed from life. It is also a raft on which to cling for substance in the world of his airy wit and his fleet-footed inventiveness. But if Shepard is intensely personal in his plays, he is also dealing with universal conditions. His *Suicide* is about everyone's need to shed the domineering past and to be free of its literalness. The mystery is how to do it. The mystery of methodology is the reason for the play's subtitle: *A Mysterious Overture*. Again, as in *Geography of a Horse Dreamer*, Shepard is mimicking the mystery genre (this time his heroes are more Peter Sellers and Inspector Clouzot than Humphrey Bogart and Sydney Greenstreet), and again the mystery has other meanings—in *Geography of a Horse Dreamer* it could be a medieval form of illumination; in *Suicide in B♭*, it is linked to the music of the senses, to an overture.

Having set up the mystery—how to reconstruct the "imagination of it" and how to find the technique to kill the disease of the past—that is, the obsessiveness with the meaning of the past—Shepard then moves his characters into play. Pablo and Louis are detectives trying to figure out the mystery—is the dead man dead? Is he "lying low" but not lying dead? Is he lying? If he's dead, was it suicide? Or was it murder in the artistic degree? Pablo seems the hard-bitten detective at first, while Louis takes as companions to himself on his detectifying pursuits newfangled intellectual theories. The man whose "death" they are investigating is the famous musician Niles, who bestrode the musical universe. (Later Niles will be the familiar Shepard character in fear of having lost his talent.) While the detectives are in the midst of their zany investigations, Petrone walks in. He plays a saxophone whose music no one can hear. This motif of sound and silence runs throughout the drama; music is salvation to those who hear it.

When Petrone cannot help the detectives solve their mystery, Pablo turns to his own theory for elucidation: Niles has been sucked up by evil forces, the forces of greed who exploited his talents and turned an innocent good American into a political and moral deviant. Shepard's satire of, and real animus against, conventional bourgeois morality takes off here as well as in the monologue by the other detective, Louis. The satire is the artist's weapon against the artist's fears of a hostile society. It reveals Shepard's awareness that he has crossed a border and lost a supporting group, the group that never felt threatened by him until he went public with his talents.

The next character who enters is Laureen, who, as an ally of Petrone, mouths the slogans of the independent artist. Her credo is that the artist needs no other force but himself in his journey into the creation of art. In a comic reprise, she says there is no need for

Niles to kill himself in order to make a statement because no audience exists to hear his statement. The artist, in Laureen's view, works in a medium of sound that only he, the artist, can hear. Shortly after her "overture," Niles and Paulette appear onstage. Niles is not dead, though he has blown his face off before the beginning of the play. But, as the dialogue between Niles and Paulette shows, reality is what one makes of it: death is not a fact unless one believes in it as fact. What Niles must do, in consequence, is to kill the burdens of his past imagination in order to take on a new imaginative force.

Niles is reluctant to enter into the planned offensive, but Paulette forces the issue. One by one, the "ones" who have been "crowding" him "up" have to go, have to be killed off, for they've gotten "out of control" and taken over his life. As Paulette shoots a bow and arrow into the King of the Cowboys (Billy the Kid), the arrow pierces Louis. As Paulette shoots the man who made Niles self-conscious about his art (the Eastern critics), Pablo feels the wound. Through all of these "plays" the characters talk about voices coming at them, voices in their heads. The import of the language is that artists and visionaries must hear their own voices, make their own sounds.

Niles is at this point pressured by Petrone into returning to the scene of the crime, that is, to the place of his own killing. Petrone is a friend from the old days, someone who knows where Niles really "lives," who knows that Niles was tripped up, entrapped into a system of false values. To find some way to return to a fresh system, Niles follows Petrone inside, but Paulette deserts him at the front door. She fears the other characters inside the house; she fears Niles will be torn apart by them (as she has torn parts of Niles from himself).

Inside the room, with Laureen, Petrone, Louis, and Pablo, Niles makes his curtain call. He restates the issue: is he alive or dead? Is he being asked questions or is he being asked for answers? Or, for that matter, is he being asked for questions, since the right questions are not so easy to find. His conclusion is that all the people inside the room are using him to project their own fears, fantasies, "criminal instincts," but then he adds a coda. A man died here a while ago, he says, and his death needs reparation.

In Niles's final speech Shepard is expressing the need to move forward, yet he fears the act of doing so—that is, he fears the loss of the comfortable, if repressive, past.

Another of Shepard's plays written during this period but not unveiled at the Magic Theatre was *Seduced,* which was given its first production by the Trinity Square Repertory Company in Providence, Rhode Island, in April 1978. It opened in New York at the American Place Theatre on February 1, 1979, with Rip Torn, who had been one of Shepard's teenage idols, in the lead role. Another of Shepard's idols, Jack Gelber, who had made theater history with his production of *The Connection,* was the director.

In *Seduced* Shepard is exposing the tragic foolhardiness of a man like Howard Hughes who thought he could rule a world from his castle in the sky (always he lived on the top floor of a hotel, or in a mountain home, or flew above ordinary mortals in his jet plane). Shepard gives to his protagonist, Henry Hackamore, the name of a rope device, *hackamore,* designed to break horses; the resulting image is one of power and ability to constrain and manipulate other creatures.

Typical of Shepard, in this and other plays, is the reuse of a word, idea, or device in works stemming from a particular time or cluster of mood. In *Fool for Love,* a later play for example, the young cowboy hero will play hackamore tricks on the bedpost of the woman he is attempting to seduce.

Henry Hackamore has created his own legend out of the success he has achieved as an aviation pioneer and as a movie producer. He has scaled the heights with his solo flying achievements, his direct involvement in business deals, and in his personal production of movies. He has, in addition, had more sexual conquests of beautiful women than any other twentieth-century man (or so he boasts). At various times during the top point of his career/achievement/life, he has withdrawn to various eyries, but below him always throb the sources of his empire, Las Vegas gambling money and California airplane technology. He touches nothing without first cleaning it with Kleenex, or a paper towel. He looks like an emaciated refugee victim, or as in the stage directions, an Indian fakir. He wears a pair of baggy white shorts and nothing else; his hair flows in a tangle below his shoulders, and his nails are pointedly long. In his mind he remains king of all he surveys, though he knows his death is near. He is aware of his mortality at the same time he denies it in his bouts of megalomania. He has instructed his trusted servant, Raul, to order a jet to bring two women to his lair on a Mexican mountainside. The women are from his past—one is Luna, who loves him in her way; the other is a dumb blonde chorine, Miami, who is the image of the starlets he acquired and tossed away in his youthful, macho days, and several of whom he turned into stars for a brief period of fame.

Luna and Miami are made to act out for Hackamore the stories of their rise to the petty rungs of stardom Hackamore has helped them reach. Luna fulfills her task by performing the story as if it were written by Hackamore; with such freedom from the hobbling of facts, the story rises to dream-vision artistic strokes. This method of fantasy is the kind of narrative play Hackamore wants. It suits the rationale of his flight from the world below him, it justifies his enclosure in his walled domain in the sky.

Hackamore expressly shuts out daylight and sun: no such light is allowed into his universe. When he travels, as on rare occasions he will have the urge to return to one of his scenes of triumph (Las Vegas is used as such a symbol), he travels in the *dead* of night in order to mask his movements from the nature of time. But Hackamore has gone beyond his wildest dreams: he no longer can separate the dream from the reality of the place he inhabits or the bodily form in which he is enclosed from the version of himself he has wrought by his will. The games he has played are beginning to bore him, and sometimes he is frightened by the revelation he finds in his own ploys. When Luna and Miami perform their stories for him under his direction, he becomes frightened of what they are saying. Abruptly he orders his servant Raul to fly them away. Just as he sent for them without warning (and expected them to comply immediately, without consideration of their schedule), he sends them away peremptorily.

The knowledge of the fact of fantasy becomes the play's motif, for Hackamore has been seduced by his own dream, just as much as Luna was seduced by the idea of Hollywood fame and Miami was seduced by the glitter of Las Vegas and the nightclub strip of neon messages. Hackamore has tried to break away from the awareness of the prison he has built for himself, but in creating a germ-free environment, he has denied life altogether. The climax occurs when Raul decides to stop playing games for Hackamore. For a long time Raul has been master of the situation, but he did not strip away Hackamore's illusions of power. Now Raul decides to make Hackamore aware of the fact of his loss of earthly powers. He orders Hackamore to sign a will that leaves all of Hackamore's fortune to Raul. Hackamore argues that he has already pledged Raul such a legacy, but Raul says Hackamore's words are worthless: they are written in air. Breaking one of Hackamore's intravenous needles (Hackamore needs artificial food because he will not eat any natural, germ-potential food) Raul dips it into Hackamore's bloody arm and forces Hackamore to sign a new will with his blood. Raul then attempts to kill Hackamore by shooting him. The bullets have no effect on Hackamore's frail body because Hackamore already exists only as myth; he has become the legend he has created. Hackamore begins a dance that signifies his awareness of spirit: he is an idea floating in the air, inalterable by human hands, alterable only by a succeeding legend.

It is within the realm of visionary truth to see in Hackamore another portrait of Shepard's desert-demented father, the once-proud warrior retreating into a desert hole. Shepard's father's fantasy of oasis lay in the trinkets of his trailer and desert trailer camp. Hackamore's fantastic oasis rests in the eyries of his manufactured sky above the desert sands of Las Vegas and elsewhere. As in *The Unseen Hand,* where the father figure plays a hovering thematic role, parricide occurs in *Seduced.* In the earlier and shorter play, the literal father is shot by his Ice son; in *Seduced,* the trusted, sonlike figure shoots the master he has served for years. In both plays the father figure does not die from the bullets shot into them. In *The Unseen Hand,* the father lives on into a new life in Indian legend; in *Seduced,* the idea of Hackamore floats in the air.

Music continues to play a central role in *Seduced,* as it did in *The Unseen Hand,* and as it has done since Shepard turned to it in the 1960s as an enriching source for his troubled spirit. The songs in *Seduced* are the songs of the 1930s—swing rhythms and fantasy-tuned lyrics. Hackamore cleans his body and his papers while such music plays on about him. The last minutes of the play are given over to music and to Hackamore's dance of death with life and with a life everlasting over death. Foolish as Hackamore may be, foolish as his dreams of power are portrayed by Shepard, he has triumphed over fact. The imagination of what it is like to be Hackamore is his legacy. His triumph lies in the fact that the imagination of himself has spread over the land.

In 1978 Shepard and his longtime friend Joseph Chaikin wrote two "voice" plays. Their attempt was to speak in a plentitude of voices, each speech caught in a moment of heightened emotion, and one "voice" following the other in a synchronic, chordal mode. The horizontal sequence was to provide meaning through a heard horizon of voiced quests and yearnings.

Chaikin journeyed to San Francisco for the first play, *Tongues,* in May 1978. He was well aware of his friend's aversion to flying, and he knew it would be difficult to persuade Shepard to come to New York by air. Chaikin had suffered serious heart difficulties earlier in the year (his heart condition was discovered in childhood), but he was strong enough to travel, and he looked forward to the collaboration with his younger partner. The two men had wanted to collaborate for years but had not found a mutually ripe time. They had been introduced at a dinner party in Greenwich Village in 1964 and become immediate friends. Chaikin was the director and founder of the Open Theater at the time, and the young and relatively unknown Shepard attended some of the Open Theater workshops. Shepard did not agree with all Open Theater principles, and he had reservations about some of its stagings. Nevertheless, he employed Open Theater actors for his play, *Icarus's Mother* and he wrote three monologues—"Cowboy," "Stone Man," and "Teleported Man"—for an Open Theater project, *Terminal*. The monologues were not used in the production that reached the stage, but Shepard later published them in his collection, *Hawk Moon*.

Shepard had no reservations in his respect for Chaikin's talent and dedication—better demonstrated then and now in directing and acting than in writing. For many years he referred to Chaikin as his "mentor." He and Chaikin agreed to write the "voices" as a team while Shepard alone would compose the music. The music was to be a kind of "jamming," a set of basic notes from which the musician—preferably a drummer—would create a concerted accompaniment to the playwrights' words. While the music was conceived as improvisational from a suggested base of notes, the words were to be spoken as written. The collaboration between the performer of the voice characters and the performer of the sympathetic percussionist musician was to be "loose," a matter of intuitive partnering.

Tongues was written in three weeks. Chaikin and Shepard met in various locations—a restaurant, a truck, a beach, their hotel room, a park. Each place became a "placing" of the voice and its shaping cry for meaning of one's place in the world of human behavior. Sometimes Shepard and Chaikin created the "voice" out of an imposed setting—that is, their own conception of character-in-milieu; sometimes they listened to voices in places in which they were meeting and then recorded the spoken words and silences they had overheard, changing them only for the rhythm of the integrated work. Sometimes the words of the voices came from a memory Chaikin or Shepard had sheltered and then allowed out into admitted consciousness, as in Chaikin's remembrance of his brother's unending reserve of proper behavior even in the most passionate of situations.

Tongues may be described as Shepard's and Chaikin's attempt to give coherence to the babble of the world through a synchronization of music and feeling; the work can also, and concurrently, be seen as issuing out of Chaikin's transformation exercises. For Chaikin had taught his Open Theater students to transform their acting selves into the essence of their character's character, and to forget about such linear and vertical details of placement as physical setting and history. In *Tongues* the essence of each emotion is expressed in the mode by which a lyric poem makes its affect: the words are meant to make the viewer/reader/hearer engage in the imagination of them rather than to provide a definition of the concerns presented. One of the overriding concerns, to which the script returns in different "voices," is death, whether as the final gasp of a body, a relationship, or a disenchantment with one's prior feelings. The "returns" are not sequential nor linked by a repeated symbol, but are connected by motifs of expression just as in a musical piece.

Although Chaikin had to return to New York, he and Shepard experienced no sense of pressure in the three-week deadline they had imposed on themselves. Like old friends dying to tell each other the stories grown during their absences from each other, Shepard and Chaikin wrote steadily and finished their script and musical notation in the allotted time. They felt good about their achievement and about their comradeship.

Chaikin was not able to return to San Francisco for a year because of his theater work in New York and in Israel and also because of his health problems. That following summer Shepard met him again at the airport and drove him to a hotel. Shepard wanted to work in one location on the new piece, so as to distinguish this collaboration from the earlier one. Consequently, most of the sessions were held in Chaikin's hotel room or Shepard's house.

Their new play was centered on one emotion—love in its various guises. Chaikin improvised on suggestions given him by Shepard, Shepard took notes, wrote versions for Chaikin to examine, and the two worked together on the final draft. Shepard insisted on the title he had suggested, *Savage/Love,* a title that irked Chaikin but that he later came to see as inspired. For *Savage/Love* is about the savagery that love inflicts on body and soul; there is nothing politic in the emotion of Shepard's conception of it or in his transformation of it in his work. Yet the play is not profoundly about violence, though often the "killing" of love becomes a central concern in it. The motif of "killing" one's love, whether through intention, perversity, or ignorance, runs through the play and provides the "savage" emblem of its title.

Like its predecessor, *Savage/Love* is a word-and-music play, in which music is integral to the form. In a program note for the San Francisco production of the two plays, Shepard wrote that *Tongues* and *Savage/Love* were attempts "to find an equal expression between music and the actor" (quoted in Marranca, 145). In the second play, however, Shepard conceived the music as instrumental rather than as solo performance, and a three-man group is suggested.

Tongues and *Savage/Love* opened in a double bill in New York at the Public Theater in November 1979. It was praised widely, and particularly by Mel Gussow, in the *New York Times,* who wrote that the performance was a "consolidation, a précis of the work of these two extraordinary theatre artists over a span of 15 years."

Five years after *Savage/Love* and *Tongues* were produced on a double bill in New York, Chaikin suffered a stroke on May 7, 1984, while in an operating room for open-heart surgery. His family and friends helped him in his recuperation; Shepard, who had come East earlier in the year to teach playwriting courses in Cambridge, visited him at his Westbeth artists complex apartment in Greenwich Village in August of that year. Partly as a way of therapy (it was Shepard whose concern conceived the idea) and partly because of Shepard's battle with his holy ghost of a father (the father had died a year earlier) and with himself as a fallen angel–prodigal son, the two collaborated again. This time they chose only one voice for their work, to which they gave the title *The War in Heaven: Angel's Monologue* and which they called a radio play with music. According to its printed cover leaf, it was first produced for radio over station WBAI in January 1985. Chaikin acted the "Voice" and Shepard performed the music.

The work is a long dramatic poem or verse play of narrow lines encompassing a depth of intensity in its shorn lineage. Not a narrative, it lacks any reference other than its associational title to a battle of angels or to the Miltonic fall of Satan. It is a lament by a "voice" for a time lost as a result of being born. The first lines denote the tone: the persona-voice declares he died on the day he was born. Shepard and Chaikin thus reverse the conventional order:

human birth is angel-dying, or heaven-exiting, and each year spent on earth is a further death from Heaven. The writers are explicit in having the persona declare that he died forty deaths (Shepard had just turned forty). Lyricizing his loss, the persona nevertheless holds onto some sense of mission about his presence on earth, but that sense of mission is soon engulfed in doubt and confusion. The persona says he does not know "exactly" where he fits in; he feels his "connections" have been broken, and his directions scattered into a thousand meaningless paths. Even his mission to retrieve the soul of a great man has proved a failure, though the failure was not of the persona's making, for he and others who had died had looked everywhere for the great man's soul but it was nowhere to be found.

The persona cries out to be taken where he was "first found" so that he can regain his power and "find his way back." Grief is one of the key notes in the persona's voice, pervading the tone of his plaint. It is not difficult to imagine that Shepard is expressing some form of grief at his father's death when he writes: "I can't live / without you imagining me / I have no life / without your thought of me." The lines may also refer to any of his loved ones (and to Chaikin's), those who gave sustenance through their substantial presence. Yet the persona's voice pleads to be let loose so that he can become his own being. It is in this repeated cry for unbinding that the paradox of the plea becomes apparent: the persona cannot become himself unless he is "imagined" by others; by himself he is nothing, yet he cannot become himself until his own views take priority over the windows of his beloved shades. Living (or active) love, the persona says, is the way to bridge the paradox, to join one being with another in the creation of a polarity that allows the unity of universe while retaining the distinction of each being. This love may be attained through "sex in soul," through the touching of "someone else," and also in the feeling between two animals, or animal and man, or in one's feeling towards God, even in "jerking off," and, lastly, in music, which "will clear the air."

The apostrophe to music however does not banish the play's coda, a repetition of the opening lines in which the voice claims his ownership of loss: he died the day he was born, and his present location is a result of some cosmic error.

The richness of the verse play has its talents in incantation and imagery. Though sound suggests the direction of thought and sense, more is invoked than meets the ear. The war in Heaven is the war in each man's soul between the life and death of human/animal/

godlike relationships. Shepard's play can be assumed at one level as an attempt to pay homage to a loved enemy, a father who failed his son but left him with the soul of a legacy. While such a love—son to dead father—is eminent domain of echo in the poem's plea, other loves may also come to mind, or to sound in the mind of memory. The love of a person newly met, a relationship that offers hope for a new beginning, is just as much a presence in the lines, and Shepard may well have been thinking of Jessica Lange, with whom he had begun living on a ranch in New Mexico. Both had suffered the pain of previously unhappy lives, each seemed to offer sustenance to the other in a possible future of redeeming mutuality. The love and grief expressed may also be Chaikin's response to his own grave situation and to his passing through it. No matter which particular referents, *The War in Heaven* is a lament for that territory of love that inhabits the land of memory from the day one is born into the awareness of loss.

Shepard had achieved a certain measure of happiness in his meeting with Jessica Lange by 1982, and he had become a major film star as a result of his role in *The Right Stuff*. He continued to work with the Magic Theatre in San Francisco, where he had achieved a second success after his self-exile in England. In *Fool for Love*, first produced at the Magic Theatre on February 8, 1983, with Shepard directing and the two lead roles played by Kathy Baker and Ed Harris, Shepard objectified his search for passage through experience to a measure of maturity. The play moved to New York in May 1983 and had a long and popular run at the Circle Repertory Company. It was made into a movie, with Shepard playing the lead role of Eddie; Shepard also wrote the screenplay for director Robert Altman.

In plot sequence the play is a narrative of two lovers—one a cowboy stunt man who has been injured enough physically to walk on a permanent limp-line through life but whose spirit refuses to die; the other is his half-sister, whose passion for her lover-sibling refuses as well to die. They leave each other, find each other, kick each other, and never forget each other. In the short span of time in which the play unfolds its dramatic action, Eddie has traveled more than a thousand miles to see Mae, who has run away from him and now lives in a dumpy motel. Mae works as a waitress and is supposedly on the way to starting a new life without Eddie. When Eddie shows up, she rejects his advances verbally and physically; at the same time she holds onto the line of contact between them.

Two rivals, one for Eddie, one for Mae, are in the background. Eddie has a countess in a Mercedes Benz waiting outside the motel room; she has followed Eddie in his thousand-mile trip. The premise is absurd (a millionaire countess obsessed with a broken-down, overage cowboy), but it makes for good fun and continues one of Shepard's appealing fantasies for men: that of being pursued as sexual object.

The countess shoots up Eddie's truck while he's inside the motel room with Mae. She is making her anger known; later she will make it more known as she sets fire to his truck. The countess is offering Eddie the opposite of what Mae offers him: Mae had given Eddie her allegiance and love, while the countess offers money, glamour, and a spitfire excitement. Mae also has a rival in store for Eddie; he is the opposite of the countess—a sweet, gentle man named Martin, who possesses the one quality Eddie lacks completely, and for which Mae yearns: a willingness to give himself completely in commitment to a person and an engagement in life. However, while Martin does not stray, he is forgetful—he has, for instance, forgotten to water the lawn of the high school where he works as a custodian. He is late for his date with Mae because he has had to turn back to do his duty on the high-school grounds.

Martin is passive, kind, and decent; the countess is impulsive and temperamental, she will shoot anything in sight to get her man and her goal. Shepard's use of horses is interesting in this play, for Eddie brings his horses in a van with him in his quest to find and retrieve the missing Mae. The countess spitefully frees them as she shoots up Eddie's truck. In this later play, *A Lie of the Mind,* the heroine's father will bring down a truckload of mules with him when he goes to visit his daughter in a hospital. He plans to sell them while visiting his gravely ill daughter; that way his trip will partly pay for itself. The use of horses in both incidents—and the tie-in to Shepard's gimmick in *Operation Sidewinder* of a couple who are getting divorced but decide to go to Reno together to get a joint vacation out of the trip—shows that Shepard does not let go of a good idea once he has used it. His continual use of several narrative ploys reveals a pattern in his thinking and attitude that suggests profound meaning in his seemingly random quips and minor plot devices. In some way, the use of the horses in *Fool for Love* and in *A Lie of the Mind* suggest a biographical relevance, a memory of an event that meant more to Shepard than to his father, to whom the events probably refer. The meaning for Shepard of these memories goes beyond the play, and are a reference *beyond* the play into Shepard's view of life. That is what makes their recurrence so fascinating.

All during the action in the motel room, a familiar Shepardian figure sits at the side of the stage—a grizzled Western man, the dried-out body of the father often seen in Shepard work. Shepard added this character to the play after its first drafts were written; in that sense, the Western grizzly/father figure is an added thought to the action, a choral comment on what is going on beneath his wrinkled view. He becomes Shepard's most forgiving portrait of the father whose yearnings turned him from his real family to the isolated community of his fantasies. As Mae and Eddie tell their stories to Martin, and to each other, the old man reacts in both wonder and consternation. For Shepard readers and viewers the stories are familiar—Eddie and Mae tell different stories of their childhood, they give different portraits of their father. What is inarguable is that the father ran off from Eddie's mother and squired another family: Mae was the offspring of this latter union. Eddie and Mae fell in love in high school, not knowing they had the same father, because the father spent part of the year with one family and part of the year with his other family. When the father's second wife (or common-law wife) tracks the father down at the first wife's house, Eddie realizes the truth of Mae's genesis, but the love he bears Mae is too great for him to stop his sexual pursuit of his half-sister.

Mae's story is quite different from Eddie's, but one father is inalterable: the father is the father is the father. Mae and Eddie are thus joined—by blood, by passion, by a tie they cannot unbind. The father, speaking on the sidelines of the stage action, demands that Eddie stand up for him and declare that the father met his responsibilities, that the father's marriage with his legal wife was an impossibility to uphold, and that he, the father, has his "rights." As all the monologues unfold, the gentle Martin and swain of Mae, who knows very little of Mae's past, attempts some synthesis of the passionate, swirling stories. Martin is the steady sod of the earth (he has just watered it before coming to pick up Mae), while Eddie and Mae are the transients of the desert; like the sand grains, they blow from one place to another, they explode and fly away on the wind. Indeed, Eddie leaves the scene with the countess in her car, and Mae packs a bag as Martin watches her in stupefied amazement. In the final moment of the play the spotlight turns on the father—whom the stage directions indicate is a construct of Eddie's and

Mae's consciousness. They talk to him, but he is *not* there. Or is he, if they believe he is there? The father, in the same manner, says at the conclusion of the play that he is looking at a picture of the woman of his dreams, but there is no picture on the wall he is looking at. The wall is empty, except for the imagination of it.

The success of *Fool for Love* is the result of many qualities. The play is a rollicking feast of passion. Eddie and Mae go at and after each other in a nonstop, dizzying fashion that delights by its sheer energy and by its amazingly inventive feats of obstinacy. The dream—or imagination—sequences with the old man/father figure have a poignancy and a clarity not as easily obtainable in other Shepard plays. And the theme is romantic as possible, at least for Shepard, for it is a tale of young lovers, Romeo and Juliet escapees from warring families with the same father. Although the lovers are not capable of lasting commitment because they will not drop their option of future alternatives, they are enveloped in the presence of an overwhelming passion, a presence that suggests a kind of crazy hope for their future. For even if Eddie runs off with the countess, a move that can only insure his transience one more time, he has the lasting image of Mae to sustain his possibilities. Although Mae says good-bye to the steadiness of the stolid nice guy, Martin, she too is not completely bereft; she has her image of Eddie to sustain her, even if the sustenance comes from throwing darts into his cardboard image. The play is reassuring on this note as well as on the note of the father's dream making, or the imagination of how things can be made to seem. Eddie and Mae's resilience suggest that Shepard in this play has moved beyond the knots that prevented action, even the action of flight, in some of his earlier work. Eddie is running away, but he is running, he has movement in his life. Mae is moving as well, even if her life from town to town seems tawdry and boringly repetitive. While maturity is not on their doorstep, it may be around some corner. At the least, Mae and Eddie have the limbs to find its branches (even with Eddie's limp). The two lovers have not lost their chances at life, and the old man has resigned himself to his imagination as his soul and sole companion. *Fool for Love* becomes Shepard's least-troubled play in its comedy of passionate foolishness as well as foolish passion. The imagination of it—that is, their imagination of their capabilities—enables them to love and leave each other.

It seems of some lingering significance that Shepard left his wife O-lan after the opening of *Fool for Love* and joined in a union with Jessica Lange. Shepard's plays are often "departures" (the word has been used by various friends of Shepard when they describe events Shepard has taken from their lives) from the premise of a real, biographical situation. His newest play and his real-life act of marital separation for a new union of love suggest that *Fool for Love* is a valentine for what-has-been and an appreciation of both the past and the possible future.

7

The Family Plays

Unlike his earlier work, Shepard's family plays demanded a great deal of nurturing. Craft and memory blended into several revisions before he allowed his creations onto a public stage. Shepard began a play about his family soon after he returned from self-exile in England in 1974. He worked on the play at his Nova Scotia farm, but left it unfinished. The several drafts whistled in the wind of his yearning to see his family *whole,* to put them in a place where they would not be forgotten but where they would no longer intrude on the currencies of his perspectives. The struggle, in which as artist Shepard wrestled with demons of memory of growing up, resulted in three plays written closely together, and often grouped as a trilogy—*Curse of the Starving Class, Buried Child,* and *True West.* Shepard's more densely complex view of family life, *A Lie of the Mind,* took longer to emerge.

Curse of the Starving Class, his first family play, was produced at Joseph Papp's Public Theater in New York on March 2, 1978. In its cast were Olympia Dukakis as the mother Ella; Pamela Reed as the daughter Emma; and Michael J. Pollard in a bit part, Emerson (his role on stage lasted less than three minutes). The central metaphor of the play is food, and its lack of it—the food that feeds the sexual, romantic, sentimental, and ideal appetites as well as the stomach. The family in Shepard's play is hungry because they do not have the right food, the kind that nourishes the psyche. Metaphorically, and humorously real, they are given real artichokes when they are in need of less vegetable and more fantasmal soul growth. When the father Weston brings home bags and bags of artichokes to stuff in the family refrigerator, the import is clear. The father brought artichokes because they were on sale when he was coming home from his desert trailer in order to get his clothes washed. When no one in the family shows appreciation of his artichoking gesture, he is offended and confounded. *The family should appreciate father bringing home the artichokes.*

In some ways *Curse of the Starving Class* appears an attempt on Shepard's part to write a play in conventional form. The work falls neatly into three acts, has naturalistic characters, and moves to a recognizable climax and, for Shepard, a denouement. It bears similarity to that genre of farce in which a worldly stranger enters into the strange world of an eccentric family. There resemblances end, for Shepard presents rites of passage in unique ways. That it is Shepard's family being portrayed is apparent, for he employs specific biographical detail. The father talks about his pilot days; the sister has been saving a chicken for a 4-H exhibit on how to cut up chickens; the son and the father talk about their "short fuses" of temper; the father lives in the desert, coming home when he needs his laundry or other chores performed that he deems a woman's work.

The tone is humorous in the opening scene when the son Wesley and the mother Ella discuss the broken front door. The father Weston had torn it down the night before when he came home drunk and could not think of any other way to get inside. Almost immediately, the tone shifts to a macabre note, as Wesley tells, in a manic monologue, of his vision/nightmare. His monologue speaks of death—of cars racing down the highway, of coyotes screaming in the desert, of American World War II planes in a duel with enemy planes. Wesley feels the fear of invasion—something strange and foreign—entering his body, taking away his soul. Even his "listening" becomes "afraid."

Wesley's trauma reflects the fear of several changes: he will learn, first, that his mother has sold the family farm on which he has grown up, and, second, that his father sold it, in a drunken stupor, a few days earlier to cover gambling debts. Wesley's fears are manifested in his prescient dream: he must face upheaval. So, also, must his sister, Emma, a more headstrong character than he. At the beginning of the play she is trying to lead a conventional life. She is a member of the 4-H Club and has been preparing a chicken for a demonstration on how to cut up a chicken. The knowledge of dislocation begins for her with the discovery that her mother has boiled her 4-H demonstration chicken for dinner (there was no other food in the refrigerator). When Emma complains about her loss—and of her family's betrayal of American (4-H) ideals—she gets a further drubbing: her brother pisses on her 4-H demonstration charts. The shocks are great enough for Emma to declare she is leaving home on her literally high horse. Yet when she hears her mother's admission that the house has been sold, Emma wails about that loss as well.

Shepard gives to the sister Emma some of the characteristics he has previously exploited for young male protagonists. Emma is stubborn and vital; she is temperamental and quick to action; she loves to ride her horse high and fast. She shoots up the nightclub whose owner has swindled her father out of his house—this is equivalent to the practice of justice in the West in earlier cowboy days, and the image of indignant Emma blazing her guns from her horse into the dark den of urbanized iniquity, the city nightclub, is straight out of a Western idealization of justice. Emma is also on the verge of adulthood—she is beginning to menstruate. In sum, Emma has to leave the family house, the land where she was born, now that her "bleeding" has begun; the "bleeding" is what she must face as an adult looking toward life's challenges.

Much of the play is concerned with the mother Ella's attempt to keep Emma in the house (the mother says the daughter is too young to leave). In the final scene, the mother is repeating the eternal maternal worry about the prematurity of departure of children. It is significant that the female is used for the painful parting of the ways as childhood succeeds into adulthood. The son Wesley, in contrast, does not cry out to leave, nor do his parents conceive of his departure from the farm. The daughter also has the choicest lines—it is she who wants everything: that is, to be omniscient and wave the magic wand that will cure the world of its problems. She wants to be a car mechanic who can fix everyone's car, so that they will have no chariot worries on their journeys to happiness; she wants to be a mechanic on life's vehicles. Her brother Wesley wants something else, he wants to stay put, to remain on the farm with his mother and with his father when the father decides periodically to come home. Because his horizons are already settled, Wesley does not even want to go on a trip to Europe that his mother is urging on him. It is also the daughter Emma who sees through her mother's protectionism: when the mother tells her daughter to stop dreaming of being the world's fixer, the daughter replies that the mother's advice is a device of absolution from guilt.

Ella the mother is a figure Shepard will continue to portray in succeeding family plays. She will not differ in characterological ways though she will carry other names. In this first family play Shepard inversely goes deeper into her conflicts and provides more motivation for her surrender to passivity, or a kind of sardonic fatalism. Ella fights for her family in the sense of trying to do something for her children, but she is defeated in her efforts. The house that gives meaning to her sense of family is to be sold. Ella tries to escape this inevitability by selling the house on her terms and thus gaining proceeds for a voyage to Europe. At the least, the money from the sale will be used for *something* (in her eyes), even if it is a vacation that the son Wesley says won't alter his sense of place in life. The mother does not get the opportunity to prove her son wrong, for the house has been sold by her husband before she can sell it: in a drunken stupor Weston had signed over the deed to a nightclub owner to cover gambling debts. Shepard builds a comedy around this sense of duplicitous selling, a comment on the erosion of values in the American landscape.

The use of the house and the land as images for reverberating contextual meaning becomes the third motif in the play. The mother and daughter (Ella and Emma), and the father and son (Weston and Wesley) are given echoing names, a device that suggests a tradition is being carried on, if only in name. The potential confusion is purposeful: Shepard is suggesting that father and son, mother and daughter, are carrying on the tradition to which they are subject both as adherents and as victims. Every son in Shepard's father's family had been named Samuel Shepard Rogers, including Sam Shepard before he changed his name, with only a following of Roman numerals to distinguish them (Shepard and Jessica Lange have continued the tradition in naming their second son Samuel Shepard Rogers). The father and son thus represent the continuity of an American dream predicated on a piece/peace of one's own, a land and place earned by hard work, purpose of will, and independence of mind. Their piece of land is small, but it is theirs to cherish. Though everything may go wrong with it, they still can tend it and retain the opportunity to reshape their losses and mistakes—that is, as long as they keep possession of it. Weston refuses to believe such a way of life as he has confirmed as his own has passed from his grasp. Given to alcoholic binges, he knows in his deepest hazes that things, and he, can *always* change: that is, that the American way, the opportunity to keep going in a frontier vision will not be closed off by mechanisms of history. Using this rationale in an ironic manner, Shepard has the father literally reborn: he forswears alcohol, shaves his stubbly beard, takes a hot bath and then a cold shower, puts on clean clothes, and throws away the unwashed, odiferous garments he has been wearing for weeks. He takes on the chores of washing all the dirty dishes in the kitchen, sweeping the littered floors, and cooking a hearty breakfast for each member of his family and he/she awakens. He is pulling out a sunny chair of optimism for his family to put their feet on. But the father's food and his gestures of reformation are too late for the rest of the family. The wife has lost faith in her husband's ability to reform, and the son cannot adapt to what he sees as his father's illusions. Emma, after a night in jail for shooting up the local nightclub, has returned home to say good-bye. Wesley threatens to leave as well, but he does not follow through on his statement. Indeed, Wesley had attempted to follow in his father's footsteps: he had gone so far as to repeat his father's actions, taking a hot bath, a cold shower, shaving his stubble of a beard, and repeating his father's oaths of mind-determination of reality. The discipline did not work for him. At the end of his charade, he picks up the old, dirty clothes the father has discarded. The son steps into the father's clothes; the son become the man; the son-man is the desert rat shorn of dreams. He will stay on the land, but he knows he has become a sharecropper on it. His decision to remain is to be viewed as tactical defeat rather than stoic victory. The father in the meantime has run off to Mexico to elude gangsters out to harm him for reneging on his debts.

It is not difficult to see in the workings of the plot and in the play's imagery Shepard's working out of his father's anger when the family farm was sold by the grandfather to cover debts. Nor is it difficult to see in the use of clothing by the son—that is, the putting on of the hair shirt of reality—a means of identification by association. This characteristic use of clothing as identification may also be seen in the father's reasoning that he can make a new man of himself by throwing away one set of clothes and adopting a new wardrobe of character.

This illusion—that the past can be plucked out of the present by sheer determination, by a metaphorical change of clothing—lies at the core of the play. It is the curse of the starving class, as Shepard sees it. The starving classes are those Americans whose spiritual needs—based on traditional, small-town, and farm values and on the mythos of the American West and its frontier—cannot be satisfied because the world in which they place their faith has eroded. In economic and social terms Shepard is talking about a whole class of people: the small country landowner disowned by large corporations and their lawyers who turn farms into industrial and residential tracts, and in the process change the nature of America. Shepard's allegiance is with the small landed family, for they have an illusion of an at least worthwhile dream. Yet his rational sights tell him of the inevitability of the failure of such an American dream.

Images of food, of a constantly empty refrigerator, of coyotes and desert life, and of a chicken and a lamb that are at first petted, then slaughtered, are peppered throughout the play. Shepard's inventiveness in the use of these images proves hilarious and poignant in turns. He brings the play to its moment of coherence with two other images: an eagle and a cat, and in their symbiotic relationship to each other. Early in the third act the father tells his son of how he was slaughtering sheep for market and throwing the sheeps' testes on the shed roof. The father noticed how an eagle flew onto the roof, more fiercely with each descent, to consume the testes. In a gesture of allegiance, the father vigorously threw onto the roof more and more testes. He was joining the eagle in a confraternity of men. That is the father's story. At the end of the play, when Ella and Wesley are left alone to carry on their depleted life, the mother tells a different story, or at least gives a different ending. A cat, smelling the food, climbed onto the roof. The eagle swooped up the cat and soared into the sky, intending to drop the cat to its death, but the cat dug its claws into the eagle's body and held on for dear life. Neither could win in the struggle, for in not dropping the cat, the eagle was dying from the loss of blood the cat's claws were inflicting. The creatures became a tableau of symbiosis: neither can live with the other, nor live if one of the other dies. This is the mother's story. It is her image of the curse under which she, as a member of her class, lives. She cannot flee from the husband, for she is a part of his traditional world and of the society into which they were born. She is as trapped as the husband. The difference is that the mother does not wallow in defeat.

Shepard's ending is uncharacteristically resolute. He is making a firm statement of identity with his roots as a Midwesterner/Westerner. He is identifying himself with farm and land values in distinction to urban, worldly ones. His work becomes an extraordinary journey into retrieval of the past as a means of departing from it.

Parallel to the family story is the change in American social norms and ideals as Shepard views them. He had been away from the United States for four years; on his return he suffered the shock of recognition. He inveighs in this play, as he rarely does in other work, against a specific target: that of the greed of the capitalist ethos as represented in the smart, city-clothed lawyer, Taylor. The satire is direct and sometimes cruel; Taylor has no goodwill going for him from any character (except the misguided Ella) and least of all from his creator. Shepard does however give Taylor Taylor's due. Taylor has *his* monologue in which he expresses his point of view: that it is Taylor and people like him, the economic superstructure and social infrastructure of modern capitalism, which keep the country going; that the land can only thrive in the recognition that contemporary means of cultivation of the land demand the acceptance of different values and different modes of working the land. Taylor justifies the impersonal substance of stocks and bonds, the means by which the contemporary world is balanced. A stock character, Taylor's stock is not easily dismissed by Shepard; he is a force ultimately not to be laughed at.

In 1979 Sam Shepard won the Pulitzer Prize for Best Drama for his play, *Buried Child.* The prize established his standing in the mainstream of American culture, and it provided the opportunity for wider exposure of his work. The award may well have been for his collective work rather than for this single play, though there is no denying the distinction of *Buried Child.* The play is both similar to and different from his earlier (and later) work in its content, but its singular distinction is its mix of archetypical American Gothic horror and humor with a poetic density of imagery and textured statement. The play is about the coming to terms with one's identity, principally in its young character Vince, but also in the other family members. The journey to acceptance of roots as a finality of consciousness rather than a designation of ethnic and/or chronological label is strewn with denial and resistance, but at the end of the play Vince has soulfully as well as literally come home. Indeed, just before his death, the grandfather, Dodge, wills Vince the family home with all its treasures and burdens, and with all its family residents, a cast that includes the grandmother Halie, Vince's father Tilden, and his uncle Bradley. As Vince gains his past family—the family he claims never gave him a family life in his childhood when he needed one—he surrenders his present relationship with his girlfriend Shelley. He sends her off in his own car for her trip back East. The only thing he keeps from the belongings they had taken on their journey together to his family house is his saxophone.

Buried Child has the autobiographical elements found in most Shepard plays, but the work is more independent of autobiography than any previous Shepard script. For what Shepard has achieved in the three-act play is a portrait of myth, of the journey tracing one's way home, and, in the process of the odyssey, finding one's port of call in that small plot of territory known as the family house. The destination cannot be reached, however, till all the buried secrets are uprooted.

Shepard uses the premise of a young man's returning to his family house for a brief visit while on the way to California. Vince starts from one coast, the East; his supposed journey is the other coast, the West. In between he will visit his house in the center of the country, in Illinois. Vince thinks of himself as a smart, sophisticated dude, having shorn himself of his country naïvetés; his girlfriend is a smart New York chick. In coming to the family house, they will see America in its Americana apple-pie setting. Shelley, the girlfriend, is prepared for laughs; Vince is seeking some reassurance from the family he has fled. Before these two journeyers are introduced to the middle-American milieu in the second act, the residents of the family house show themselves off to the audience. They are an odd group, anything but the sweet-coated apple pie of Vince's girlfriend's limited imagining. Dodge, the grandfather, is in his seventies and is dying; his mantle must be passed on, but his survivors do not present promising substance for the inheritors of a domain. Halie, the wife, first presented as a voice harping (offstage), is either a shallow social climber or a tactitian whose choice of illusionary perspective allows her to cope with her world of diminishing returns. Halie gets through life by forgetting its problems once she has established a routine for domestic chores and pleasures; she also flirts with the local preacher, whose unctuousness and social prejudice help to raise her own self-estimation. Halie has done her share of living in the world of the past: she has squired three sons, and possibly a fourth. She has tended to her husband, whose fondness for the bottle has often stripped him of his powers, and she has kept up the family's (or, more accurately, her own) pretensions. Tilden, Halie and Dodge's oldest son, is presented in the first act as an American Gothic retard—he hulks about in a defective manner; something is wrong with him, but the playwright never shows what *is* the matter. In Illinois he showed promise for the greatest social rewards of the three sons, for he was a fullback or quarterback on the high-school team; the actual position on the field is less important than the mythos of his brief athletic fame and the letter on his sweater (Halie for example can never remember which position her son played, though she remembers he was a star). When Tilden went to New Mexico—for reasons purposefully kept mysterious in the play—something happened to him. The "something" is never identified, but it is associated with breakdown, defeat, and probably a stay in the penitentiary. Tilden has returned home to be taken care of, a Frostian man of defeat who has come to the only place that will take him in. Bradley, the second son, has always been less promising than either of his brothers; his status is defined by his crippled condition. Bradley lost half his leg to a chain-saw accident in his youth. The mother and father must also take care of Bradley—both their sons are invalids, one without a leg, one without a full mind. Thus, Halie's dream that her children will take care of her in her old age is trampled by the accident of facts. Ansel, the third son, according to Halie, was the most intelligent of all of them, though he was not (in her words) as handsome as Tilden or Bradley. But Ansel died young, and whatever world of possibility of the son taking on the reins of the household died with his death.

Sometime after Ansel's death, and after the return of Tilden from New Mexico and Bradley's accident, another child was born in the family. This is the buried child of the play, and the central image of the play's concern. One thing is clear: if the child ever was born, it was borne by Halie. She is the mother in fancy, if not in fact, in all the legends that follow. The father's identity is less clear. At one point Tilden refers to the child as his; at another point Tilden calls the child his father's (Dodge's) child. Dodge, the grandfather, denies the child's birth, both in his part of the creation of the progeny and in the story of the creation itself. (Dodge says that the child was conceived in a time when he had not slept with his wife for six years.) None of these details deter the story, for its fascination, as in myth, lies in the appeal of the terror of the myth. If Tilden is the father of the slain and buried child, then he and his mother have committed incest. His breakdown then may be a metaphor for his punishment, a pulling out of the eyes of his psyche. If the child is Tilden's, then Dodge's killing of it is a double, or triple, or multiple murder, for Dodge has killed his grandchild, his stepson, his son, and his own wife by extension.

Whatever the origins of the progeny, Dodge says at one point that the child is not fit to be a member of the family. In his monologue Dodge deals with the unwanted fact, the intrusion of the alien unwanted, by burying it in the garden in the back of the house. If Dodge can keep the secret without being felled by its oppressive burden, Tilden cannot. The star letterman becomes the clod of the family, an invalid Oedipus wandering round the house and backyard. Halie, the wife, mother, fornicator–Jocasta figure also has escaped into a fantasy world by refusing to think about the past; she thinks about things as she has arranged to think about them. Thus Shepard's House of Atreus is as fatally and fatalistically drawn as its Greek model. For, just as Oedipus could not escape his traffic accident, so Halie and Dodge cannot escape the blow of the fourth child, whether that "child" was an actual baby or a mythic burden.

Halie had hoped to ride out the middle years of her life in comfort—she and Dodge had done their duty for family and country and were settling into a manageable life—but fate decreed another pattern.

That Shepard's narrative is conceived on a mythic plane is evidenced in the mystery surrounding the events in the play and in the lack of specific detail and plausible sequences. When the fourth baby was born is never made clear; when Tilden went to New Mexico is similarly given over to hazes of dates. That both events are indivisible from each other is manifest in the play's dynamics. Tilden's marriage, and the date of his son Vince's birth, is also shrouded in ambiguity. Is Vince a substitute for the buried child? A child might conceive just such an association for himself, particularly if the observable (as opposed to buried) child thinks himself unwanted. Is his neglect—as narrated by Vince in one of his monologues—a result of Tilden's obsession with the lost child? Just as the mysteries of information are purposeful in the play, so too are the resolutions of them. When, in the last minutes of the play, Tilden is seen carrying into the house the dirt-covered corpse of a child, the visual effects suggest physical proof of the buried child. Yet the corpselike figure Tilden is carrying up the stairs presumably to force his mother to acknowledge it can be any number of representations of meaning. It may be a vegetable, it may be a doll, it may be someone else's child. It is always the dirty secret, the buried dirt, that must be brought to the surface before it can be got rid of.

That final moment in the third act is one of Shepard's most extraordinary poetic-visual, metaphoric-dramatized effects. As Tilden, in his lame-footed and lamebrained way, is moving menacingly up the stairs to his mother's bedroom (her husband has just passed away—the father is dead, the son is approaching), she is chattering away. As in the opening scene, she is all voice—the audience did not see her before she had spoken hundreds of lines. Now in the final moments of the play she is heard from offstage talking to her husband in the usual manner, paying as usual no heed to his statements or his silences; she is cognizant only of those realities she has created for her hold on what she conceives as her sanity. She is not aware of Dodge's death, but then she has not been aware of his life for many years. She is saying that there are indeed vegetables in their garden, that the land is thriving. She has doubted her son Tilden earlier when he brought in corn and carrots for the family table. She had thought Tilden was up to his old tricks, that he was sick again. Now she agrees with her son that the garden is blooming.

The poison weed has been unearthed, she exclaims. First, she says, the bloom is due to the rain—it has rained during the first two acts of the play. Then in the last line of the play she says it is the result of the sun. Both causes of the land's rebirth, of the vegetable growth of family sustenance, are preceded by the condition of Halie's "maybe." Maybe the rain did it, maybe the sun did it, Shepard has her say in parallel incantatory monologues. Maybe Shepard is saying that growth is due both to rain and sun, that neither can replenish the earth without the other. All this while, the certainty of Tilden on the dark stairs—of his momentary breaking into the world of Halie's fantasized shelter of bedroom and forcing her to view the buried dirt he holds in his hand—moves before the viewer's eyes. The certainty of growth is inescapable, but one's reaction to it varies from character to character. Halie may survive the shock of recognition; she has after all come to accept the corn and carrots in a land she only recently called barren. Or, like Dodge, she may move onto another plane of consciousness. Her fate is uncertain, but not her grandson's.

Vince, the grandson, remains below in the house, having inherited it from his grandfather who has died moments before. In taking possession of it, he sends off his girlfriend from the East. He rejects that part of the world in which flight and running were his rationalized means for denial of family. Vince had tried to run away in the second act—he had jumped into his car and driven through the rain into Iowa, into the center of his being as the car sped along the slick road, into the high point of the center of middle America where he was born and to which he knew, at the end of the rainy journey, he was returning. Shelley, his girlfriend, had been sympathetic to his journey of self-exploration, but Vince, now master of his house, decides Shelley—the woman of the East Coast—has no place in his country life. His rejection of Shelley may be seen as one discordant note in the play, for it suggests that Vince, like his parents and grandparents, has become insular in his Middle Americanness. Even though Shelley has mocked Grant Woods, homey traditions, and the mythos of mom, pop, and apple pie, there is no proof she is incapable of growth and understanding the American way of Shepard's Midwest. For Shepard to have Vince send her off, alone in a car back to her place, suggests once again that Shepard himself shows evidence of insularity: he is tolerant of Shelley's bohemianism, but he has Vince reject it without a struggle. All of Shelley's efforts to understand him are dismissed without any exhibition of the pain of ambivalence.

Both because of its Pulitzer Prize award and its extraordinarily powerful script and effective staging, *Buried Child* proved a great success in its first production. It has continued to be one of Shepard's most popular plays. The humor of its moments when Shelley meets the typical Midwestern family are as brilliantly wacky as one gets in contemporary drama. No doubt the scenes owe something to the mode George S. Kaufman and Moss Hart established in *You Can't Take It with You,* but Shepard has honed the premise and its angles into a unique blend of fear, paranoia, and the comedy of eccentricity. The mode is particularly evident in Shepard's family plays: Taylor, the alien cold-blooded lawyer–con man introduced to the wacky family in *Curse of the Starving Class;* Frankie, the "alien" brother forced into living with the strange household in *A Lie of the Mind;* Saul, the Hollywood producer, easily fooled by the subtexts operating in the minds of the writer brothers in *True West.* Shepard works variations on the premise, as the device obviously excites his dramatic imagination.

Several other devices connecting this play to the other family plays may be mentioned. In both *A Lie of the Mind* and *Buried Child* the comic ploy of the stealing of a blanket from one character by another is used—the blanket becomes the new image for the missing food in *Curse of the Starving Class.* In addition, an artificial leg is stolen for comic effect in *Buried Child.* In all the family plays, sets of siblings are used as manifestations of aspects of character. *Buried Child* has three (or four, if the "buried child" is considered in the counting); *True West* has only two, while in *A Lie of the Mind* four pairs are employed for parallel foiling.

What may well be one of the most significant features in Shepard's family plays—that is, for an understanding of what he was attempting to understand, placate, and/or rationalize—are the parallel situations in which he places the mother character. In *Curse of the Starving Class, Buried Child,* and *True West,* destructive or constructive turns of behavior occur only after the mother has gone offstage. In *Curse of the Starving Class,* the house gets its wrecking (reckoning?) after Ella goes off with the lawyer, Taylor, and the daughter, Emma, goes off on an escapade that will land her in jail. In *Buried Child,* violence takes place in the house only after Halie has gone off with the pompous preacher; when she returns to see the effects of the violence, she says that trouble she cannot control occurs when she's not around. In *True West* the premise of the narrative demands that the mother be on a trip to Alaska so that two brothers can meet each other without amelioration of their fratricidal conflict and/or distraction of motherly concern. In parallel resolutions or working out of conflicts in the four plays, the mother's position is consistent. In all the family plays, the mothers accept the world that the men—husbands and sons—make. They rationalize the continuation of their limited world in a melody of sighing and a dance of retreat to a room of their own. In *True West* the mother goes off to a motel till the "boys"—her two sons—resolve their deadly battle. In *Buried Child* Halie goes up to her castled room (though invasion is threatened by Tilden on the stairs to the second story, but, significantly, Shepard has not yet written that second story in which the mother faces the facts). Even in *A Lie of the Mind,* when there seems a real, if limited, reconciliation of Meg and Baylor, the mother remains downstairs for a while to reclaim her feelings and her sense of self, and her husband warns her to remember her limits: she is not to disturb his dreams when she does come to his bed later.

True West, the third in Shepard's family plays, is on the surface Shepard's most realistic play, but the surface is only part of the story. The realistic setting, and the seeming realistic description and linear narrative unfolding, is emphasized by Shepard in his stage directions, where Shepard explicitly writes that no distortions in the shape of real objects or colors should be made in the setting, and no distractions should compete for the focus of the play, which is the "evolution of the characters' situation."

True West was first produced at the Magic Theatre in San Francisco in July 1980 under the direction of Robert Woodruff. It was brought to New York for Joseph Papp's New York Shakespeare Festival/Public Theater and opened there on December 23, 1980. Papp replaced Woodruff as the director after the two differed on the presentation. Shepard denounced the Papp decision to replace Woodruff but allowed the production to continue; Shepard was out of town on movie work at the time.

If Shepard chooses realism and a more conventional linear narrative as his style and mode in this play, the story beneath the observed circumstances and character has a familiar continuity in its rhetorical questioning of social responsibility and artistic endeavor. Other familiar elements are apparent in the work: the coyote, and its contrasting complement of desert life, the cricket, sound their note of attention. The two brothers, Lee and Austin, are in a sense the human parallels of the coyote and the cricket: Lee is the loner and desert rat proclaiming his fruitless independence in the dark desert air; Austin is the conscientious writer clacking/chirping away at his typewriter in his production of stories. Austin is too self-conscious to call his work "art," though such a declaration would be no more self-conscious than his denial of artistic desire and enterprise. What Austin lacks is the self-conscious commitment—the arrogance of his own worth and distinction—of the true artist. His brother Lee, on the other hand, possesses the arrogance of the artist but none of the discipline, or the desire for such discipline. Lee lacks the humility of the artist, as necessary a component of the true artist as an acceptance of the special distinction that sets artists apart from their fellow human beings.

While seemingly different, the brothers are complementary aspects of the artist. When the movie producer Saul Kimmer says he believes the two brothers are one, the ideal of the two selves of the artist is made explicit. But, as Shepard shows, the selves do not cohere—they are always at war. Lee recognizes this inalterable fact when he tells his brother that most murders are committed in the family, and most family murders are those committed by brother against brother.

The plot devices of the play are clever, and, for Shepard, highly schematized. They issue out of character and one central premise. Lee, the drifter, has turned up unexpectedly at his mother's house in Los Angeles. The other brother, the conscientious husband and son, Austin, has come down to watch the mother's house while she takes a vacation trip to Alaska. Many critics have pointed out the arbitrariness of Lee's appearance—he just shows up that day—but Lee is an arbitrary character, relying on nothing but the instincts of whim. What is not as often noticed is the improbability of Austin's situation—that he would leave his wife and children in San Francisco to attend to his mother's house for two weeks. Though it is possible that Austin likes the idea of a place all to himself so that he can write without distraction, the necessity of waiting for such an opportunity as his mother's house vacancy seems farfetched. Austin is presented as a successful writer who doesn't need money or work space. Yet, once the suspension of disbelief of the premise is accepted, the rest of the play follows inevitably. Austin and Lee will reverse their roles in life because each is seeking the other, each wants to taste the other half of life. Austin is working on a screenplay for a Hollywood producer. He gets Lee out of the house by giving him, against his better judgment, the keys to his car. Lee, a petty thief, returns earlier than his promise to stay away from the house; he has brought with him a TV set he has stolen from a house in the neighborhood. Austin had told his brother to stay away because a movie producer was coming to discuss Austin's script, but the devious Lee comes early if only to see what mischief he can cause. (Another improbability in the script is the arrival of Kimmer the producer at Austin's residence. Most Hollywood producers, especially the mogul types of which Kimmer is one representative, do not go to their writer's homes; their writers come to them—but the turnings of the plot demand that Kimmer be around to meet Lee.) Lee arranges, through his clever deviousness, a golf date with Kimmer the next morning, and during the game wins the producer over to filming Lee's script idea for a true Western. The producer is in fact so taken with Lee as the real thing, the real West man, that he puts aside Austin's script for a later production schedule.

Thus the stage is set for the true Western. Which is the right script for Kimmer to latch onto? He wants only to produce a money-maker, but he reasons that people go to the movies for the illusion of truth. He then must provide them with the truth of illusions, that is, the West they want to see because that is the West in which they believe. Austin cannot believe the producer has rejected his literate script for the amateur, hackneyed version of the West his brother Lee is presenting. Yet Lee's West may be truer than Austin's conception of the place, for Lee believes in the credo of the illusionary, traditional West—that is, he recognizes it as the real thing whether it is out of date or not. Austin has never believed in such a West; for him, it has always been a fiction, one he is willing to exploit for social and artistic advancement.

In the course of role reversal, Austin will get drunk, begin singing Western cowboy songs, and in one hilarious episode become the modern drifter-cowboy-outlaw who steals all the toasters in the suburban town in which his mother lives. While Lee has stolen only one TV set, Austin steals more than twenty toasters. In a climactic scene, as his bourgeois defenses crumble in the loss of his writing status to Lee, Austin cries out that he must go to the desert and live there like a coyote, a free scavenger. He begs Lee to take him there; he will now be Lee's subordinate just as earlier he had assumed he, as a wage-earning writer, was superior to his brother. But Lee is not so willing to take Austin back to the desert. One reason is that Lee is enjoying his new life as a writer-celebrity and he wants Austin to continue to edit the ideas/scripts he is turning out. Another is that Lee knows Austin is incapable of living in the desert or as a desert rat. Austin's notion of desert life is an illusion, lately arrived at or at least lately expressed, that romanticizes the desert just as much as the true West is disdained by Austin as an illusion. Austin believes the desert will allow him to become a man, to drop all pretenses at social responsibility, and to live a self-centered utopian life. Austin, Lee fears, would be an aberration in the desert, a creature too refined by his past to adapt to nature's demands. (The mother repeats the same fear later in the play, when she says that Austin is "too skinny" to survive in the desert.) Yet, to appease Austin and thus to keep him working away as his writing slave (ghostwriter), Lee agrees to take Austin to the desert at some later day. In jubilation Austin hands him a piece of toast he has made (Austin has put bread in every one of the stolen toasters and made himself a wealth of stolen goods). Lee finally eats the toasted bread as Austin slobbers on his leg, like a contented dog/slave.

Into the melee comes the mother, who has returned early from her Alaska vacation because she missed her plants. The plants have died because Austin has neglected them as he became like Lee, a man who thinks only of himself. The mother is astounded by the news that Lee has sold a script and Austin has not. She is astounded by the shambles of her house. She cannot believe that Austin wants to give up his family, his career, and his bourgeois comfort to go off into the desert with his brother. Yet in some way she perceives the fact of the truth: the father of the two boys, her husband, also went off into the desert, abandoning wife and family. The two boys are infected with the same dream as the father; he passed the disease onto Lee, and now Austin has contracted it. The disease/the dream is that notion of the true West and its mythos as sustenance for the "real" or macho man. The mother no longer can cope with the power of the dream that warps her men, and she goes off to a motel to rest until the boys leave. Shepard's mother character in this and in other of his family plays surrenders to a fatalism in which she acts out a traditional role of the West, just as the male characters act out theirs. The mother's traditional role is a passive one: she is the handmaiden to the man's need, desires, and dreams.

In *True West* the father does not appear physically but his presence is felt. The two brothers refer to the father several times, and they are rivals for his approval/affection. They do not verbalize their trips to the desert to see the father as a journey of homage, but their behavior and their imagery tell the truth. Each wants the father's blessing wholly. The father gives neither his blessing, because he is not capable of passing on a power that is only illusion. His patrimony exists in the mind, but in this case the legacy is more delusion than inspiration. In the desert the father is a bedouin king;

to acknowledge his sons with a resolution of approval would be to introduce the same fears and tremblings the father experienced in the world outside his desert shelter. One of the memory-accented references in the play concerns the contact each of the brothers makes with the father. Austin has given him money, and is angry because the father spent it on liquor. Lee has given his father the compliment of imitation—Lee understands the father's spurning of Austin's bourgeois-conditioned allegiances.

The father becomes the apex of the triad of the West, with the two sons, or two sides of the son, at each angle of the triangle. The play does not resolve the question of the true West—Los Angeles or Needles, California, urban house or Mojave Desert trailer, social conformity or independent drifting—but it presents the conflict in one of Shepard's most haunting, and frightening, images. As the play ends, the two brothers are alone on stage, at each other's throats, each blocking the other's way out of the room, each poised to kill the other. The question that arises and remains long after the brilliantly frightening image is the one of wonder whether Shepard is presenting a mythic drama in which one brother must kill another in order to survive, in which the artist, in all his guises, and the responsible citizen, in all his working shifts, must continue to war with each other. Though Bertolt Brecht's influence on Shepard was long ago absorbed into Shepard's unique view of things, the ending of *True West* has a Brechtian air of epic alienation.

Under Shepard's direction *A Lie of the Mind* appeared in New York at the Promenade Theatre on December 5, 1985. The director was Shepard, and in the distinguished cast were Harvey Keitel, Amanda Plummer, Aidan Quinn, Geraldine Page, and Will Patton. In the published text Shepard specified two offstage properties. (1) There had to be a musical accompaniment to the dramatic proceedings, but it was to be more than merely accompaniment, it was to be a choral chord of communication with the narrative. The Red Clay Ramblers were the musical performing group in the original New York production, but Shepard did not demand their exclusive employment for the play. (2) The settings were to be as spare as possible. Only a few props and pieces of furniture were to be used. No walls were to appear on stage. The suggestion of empty space was to be achieved by the enormity of the wall-less world on stage. The effect of "bare space" was to be suggested by lighting that played off dark against bright space. Ramps and platforms as well as the stage floor were to serve as levels for the states of mind and physical actions of the characters.

Shepard's demand for music as an integral part of the production was the culmination of his work with country music and rock groups. In *A Lie of the Mind* he created a kind of musical play that, contemporary as it is in feel, substance, and musical reference, harks back to traditions of earlier centuries—the echoes of the medieval church and communal plays may be heard in it. Shepard's demands for atmospheric physical settings without walls are indicative of expressionist and Beckettian techniques of stagecraft, but they also hark back to an earlier century and mode. In Elizabethan and Shakespearian drama few properties and no walls were employed on stage. A particular tapestry, piece of furniture, and/or a few additional physical objects were adequate to suggest a world. Like Elizabethan stage characters, Shepard's figures move through time and space through "the imagination of it."

The play opens with a phone call from Jake to his younger brother Frankie, saying that something terrible has happened. Jake's wife, Beth, is dead, he says. The declaration is an overstatement as the second scene/tableau will reveal. Jake has beaten his wife savagely and senselessly, but she is alive and recuperating in a hospital in Los Angeles. She is brain-damaged, as becomes evident in her conversation with her brother Mike. In the third scene/tableau Frankie has brought his brother Jake home to their family apartment; Jake is still in a state of shock over what he has committed. In Jake's telling of it, Beth deserved her beating because she was "fooling around" with men from the drama group/amateur acting company whose classes she attended. Jake says Beth teased the men and provoked him, Jake, into punishing her for her transgressions. When Frankie asks Jake if he has reported Beth's death to the police, Jake says there is no need for the police—they can no longer help. Jake remains convinced he has done the right and proper thing. Frankie suggests that Jake's behavior is characteristic of him, and of his famous past temper: he once kicked the innards out of a pet goat because the goat had stepped on Jake's feet. Sensing the truth of his brother's comment, Jake begins to tremble. In compassion for his brother's suffering, Frankie tells him he will find out what really has happened to Beth.

In the next scene Beth's brother Mike is helping his sister walk around the hospital corridor. She is in better shape than in the previous scene, but she remains an ailing mental and physical invalid. Beth repeats her broken assertions that Jake has killed both himself and herself. In her new, childlike condition, Beth states the profound insight of the murder of their love, an insight into the recognition that Jake is "her heart."

In this first act Shepard is alternating scenes between members of the two protagonist's families—Beth's and Jake's. The next scene shows Jake in his mother's apartment. He is like a child again to her, and she is making a tremendous fuss over her little boy, to whose needs she must minister. Jake's sister, Sallie, who lives with her mother, is now shunted aside by the mother. Jake, however, pursues his sister as if she were his wife Beth. Jake's pursuit is an aggressive one, and Sallie is frightened by it. When the mother declares that she is going to take Jake into the apartment to nurse him back to health, Sallie threatens to leave. The mother not only ignores her threat but prods her daughter to consummate the words.

Predictably, in scene 6, Beth's family will now be delineated. Beth's parents are polar opposites of Lorraine, Jake's mother (the father has disappeared into the desert). Beth's father is more concerned with his horse business than with his daughter's critical health problem. Beth's mother is vague and passive in the face of her husband's self-centered demands. The father is, for example, annoyed that Beth is asleep when he enters her room; he has, after all, traveled thousands of miles from Montana to the big city hospital in Los Angeles. However, the father reasons, all is not lost, because he has brought a team of mules with him in his van: he will sell them while he is in Los Angeles. (The ploy and black humor of this material is reminiscent of the couple in *Operation Sidewinder* who are getting a divorce and decide to take a joint vacation to Reno, since they have to be there anyway for the legal proceedings.) Beth's father refuses to wait until Beth wakes up. Besides, as he says, if Beth is brain-damaged, there won't be much to talk about. And when his son Mike tells him that he, Mike, is planning to drive Beth back to the ranch in Billings, and would like his mother to accompany them, serving as a backup nurse for Beth, the father is annoyed. He had counted on the mother's company on the long trip back home, and now he'll have to drive it all alone. Meg, the wife, cheerfully offers a consolation: there's "good radio between here and Billings, Dad," she says. Baylor, the father, reluctantly accepts the loss of his wife's companionship, but he remains unconvinced about the wisdom of their participation in the journey with Beth.

In scene 7, Jake's mother Lorraine is feeding soup to Jake. She tells her son that Beth is not worth his worry. When she lets slip that Frankie has gone to Montana to ascertain Beth's condition, Jake grows frantic. He knows Beth's condition is his problem to identify; Beth's condition is his world, his universe, and he should be in it. He begins to look for his pants but cannot find them (Lorraine, the mother, in anticipation of such a turn of events, has hidden them). Lorraine tells her son that he should never have left his room in the first place. This room was a haven after all the wanderings they, mother and son, made with the father from airbase to airbase during World War II. The references to Shepard's autobiographical experiences, and to his father's service in the army air force, is patent and suggests that Shepard sees a part of himself in Jake: the man who smashes things when the pressure is too great to bear.

Jake's character is much like Jeep's in *Action,* a being who cannot accept a chair offered him or the tabling of his passion, and who breaks chairs instead of breaking bread with his mate. The association with Shepard's father, and by extension with Shepard, is made deeper when Jake demands to see the box in which his father's ashes lie. The mother had stashed the box under Jake's bed years ago, and now it is pulled out. In the box are an American flag and the father's war medals. Yet, as the mother says, the father did not die a hero: he was killed by a truck on a highway. (The reference to the truck on the highway is a clue for resonance with the scene in *True West,* when it is revealed that the father figure died in an alcoholic haze when he could not move from the middle of the highway as a truck was bearing down the road.)

Act 2 will move from the world of Jake's Los Angeles to Beth's Montana. Now at her family home, Beth is recuperating. The brain damage is permanent, but limited: Beth can understand certain problems and relationships, and she has selective memory. While she is puttering about the house, Jake's brother Frankie is trying to get into it to apologize for his brother's deed. Beth's brother Mike has kept Frankie from fulfilling his goal, and sent him on his way, but Frankie has got lost in the woods, and as he jumped through a bush trying to find his way, he had been shot by Beth's father Baylor. Baylor brings Frankie into the house (he owes him some hospitality after shooting him); it is the father's way of apologizing for thinking Frankie a deer. The treatment accorded Frankie inside the house becomes the comic centerpiece of the act, both as display of Shepard's brilliant wit and as thematic development. Baylor tells Frankie that he had better not sue him (Baylor informs the wounded man that he'll get his ass kicked if he brings any big-city lawyer ways into Montana). Mike wants the man who can't move his leg to get a move on. Beth wants to take care of the man, whom she sees as the opportunity for revising the wounds of the past. Meg is vaguely maternal and maternally vague about the goings-on; she keeps on hoping everything will turn out fine.

In the third scene of the second act Shepard gives to Beth the ironic-comic touch of telling her family that everything that has happened to them will soon become acceptable to them. Beth announces that everything can turn around in a second: it is a matter of which way one looks at the circle. Since everyone has been tending Beth in the hope she will get well, her response is only fitting: she is trying to please her well-wishers. In the following scene Shepard returns to Los Angeles and to Jake's mother and sister. Lorraine is also trying to convince her son that everything will be all right, if Jake just stays home with his mom. Lorraine blames her daughter Sallie for returning to the apartment when there is no longer room for her; besides, as the mother points out, Sallie left voluntarily in a huff over her mother's preferential treatment of the son and nothing in that situation has changed. Lorraine simplifies the issue by calling her daughter a troublemaker. Later that night Jake will escape his mother's net of concern by getting his sister Sallie to sleep in his bed while he escapes into the night, with only his father's flag and his own underwear to carry him through his hegira to Montana. Fifteen hundred miles away in Montana, Beth will wake up screaming as Jake leaves his room through the open window in Los Angeles. Just as earlier Beth had said that Jake had murdered their love in his beating of her, so Beth feels the pain and the spur of Jake's journeying. Each is a symbiotic part of the other, each is joined in union with the other, no matter how many geographic miles separate them. Beth's primal scream is the climax of the play, though far away from its many strands of resolution.

In the third act, when Lorraine discovers the ruse of her daughter in her son's bed, she explodes into anger. She accuses her daughter of being a party to the killing of the father who had run off to the desert. Lorraine is doubly angry at the new loss of her son—Jake is still a part of her though he left her years ago, and the new loss brings back the memory of loss of her husband, the errant man who has been dead for many years. In her own defense Sallie declares she did not kill her father; if anyone is responsible for his death, it is Jake, she says, since Jake took the father, a recovering alcoholic, into a bar in Mexico—the father was living in a desert outpost in the neighboring foreign country, and the son and daughter had journeyed down to see him. He had welcomed them in his cluttered trailer home, he had shown them pictures on his trailer wall: there was one of Jake running with a football, another of Jake in the 4-H Club. Jake was all over the wall, as were Gene Autry and Ginger Rogers. The family pictures on his wall were the family he wanted, and the family that his imagination could lead him to conceive. What the father had done was ingenious and philosophically resolute: he made his family out of pictures, rather than made snapshots out of his family. Thus Shepard's father proved again the efficacy of the imagination, its force as an insight into the perceptions of the individual eye. However, Jake's reaction to his father is not so easy to understand. He turned vicious, spurring the old man on to drink after drink in a contest the son knew he had to win over an ailing father. Jake bet his father that whoever could drink in every bar from the father's trailer habitat to the Mexican-US Border would win the challenge. Thus Jake's bet with his father was an act of parricide, as clearly a killing of the father as the one in *The Unseen Hand*. In this scene, if not also throughout the play, Jake's consciousness of act suggests Shepard's perception of desire—the son who must renounce/denounce the father in order to break free from him. The psychological-symbolic aspects are manifested in Jake's stealth and in the father's vulnerability that nevertheless refuses to back down from a macho challenge thrown by his son, a real killer of a guy. Lorraine will accept none of these Freudian implications and Electra allusions from her daughter; indeed, in self-defense against her own possible breakthrough of knowings, she will accuse her daughter of being the father's murderer because Sallie did not drag her dead-drunk father from the highway as the truck was closing in on him. In addition, the mother asks why Sallie did not drag the wounded father to their car and drive him to a hospital. Sallie, in thorny triumph, nails the deed on Jake: Jake, she answers, had the car keys.

Sallie's defense dampens the mother's rhetoric, and the mother admits to the destructiveness of the love game. Once begun on the etiology of family feeling, Lorraine cannot stop: she is going to get rid of Jake's model planes and the father's model planes. The father was a dreamer, a hopeless one. Lorraine is going to surrender his hold on her.

In scene 2, as part of Shepard's dramatic pattern, the setting shifts back to Beth's parents' house in Billings. The wounded Frankie is asleep on the couch—he has been fighting to get his share of a blanket to keep himself warm, but the father Baylor also covets the blanket. The father believes he has more right to the blanket than the stranger, Frankie. Blanket stealing is a comic technique Shepard uses in several plays, notably this one and in *Buried Child* where the blanket plays the symbolic role of warmth and security, and its theft represents the loss of that warmth and the betrayal of love by family members.

The family scene in Montana is rendered in a comic vein. As Frankie nurses his bloody leg, Meg is putting mink oil on her husband Baylor's foot because he's been out hunting. It is a loving wifely gesture that leads Meg to relax and to talk with her husband in an affectionate manner. Baylor refers to Meg's mother as a nut, someone who went insane and had to be put away, but Meg says it wasn't a case of insanity, it had more to do with being male and female. The remark falls on the unhearing ears of the mentally deficient Beth, hovering on the scene. When the women leave the room, Baylor tells Frankie, now almost white from loss of blood, that he is to expect no easy life in the house: he'll have to do his share of work, earn his keep while he is recuperating. Baylor wants Frankie to help him put on his socks, because it's hard for Baylor to get them on. Frankie's injured leg is not to be used as an excuse for getting out of this assignment. Baylor claims he isn't being mean, he's just acting the way a man ought to act—he hunts deer, for example, because it's deer season. If a man gets caught in the crossfire of a hunting gun's proper explosion, that is part of the hazards of being a man. Frankie, at this point, only wants to go home: he tells Baylor that his brother Jake will soon arrive and rescue him. His brother Jake, Frankie says, has a "short fuse."

Frankie's desire to get away from the family clutches in Billings runs into a new obstruction: Beth has decided she wants to marry him. (Beth makes the announcement against the backdrop of distant hunter's gunshots.) In response to Beth's proposal, Frankie tells her that he cannot betray his brother by taking his wife from him.

Beth's brother Mike walks in on the two of them to announce he has just taken Jake prisoner. The wife beater had made the successful trek to Billings, but Mike had captured him before he could enter the house. Mike has beaten Jake so thoroughly (the poetic justice to equal Beth's beating) that he has got Jake to apologize for all the wrongs he has done; Jake has become a new man, a repenter, or rather a penitent dog. Mike announces that he has trained Jake to act like a dog, ready to apologize whenever Mike raises his hand; Jake is a licker of wounds now. Yet, for all his labors of love, Mike finds no one is paying him much attention. Meg and Beth are interested in other matters—preparations for the wedding of Frankie and Beth. What a wonderful thing a wedding is, the two women say to each other. They begin indulging in the dream of a beautiful wedding and its value to the imagination of those who dream on it.

Shepard brings his viewer/reader back to Los Angeles in the next scene. In contrast to the coming union in Beth's Montana, the disintegration of family and roots is evident in Lorraine's and Sallie's preparation for their trip to Ireland. Lorraine has thrown out the recent past and is packing her bags for a trip to the Old Country, where she hopes to find a remaining relative of her family. She is sure there is one relative left, one "straggler," who did not die off, and she is sure someone in a little Irish village will lead her to that family member. Lorraine's trip is the same kind of trip Ella was planning to take in *Curse of the Starving Class* when she made her preparations to sell the family farm and find new roots in an "old land" in Europe.

As Lorraine begins burning mementoes of the past that she has saved for years, a flame light bursts over the stage, and the scene shifts to Montana. On all fours, dressed only in his underwear, Jake is performing like a dog for Beth's brother Mike: the father's American flag Jake has carried all the way to Montana has been rolled up into a log and placed between Jake's teeth for the good dog to carry. Mike is Jake's master, leading him on an imaginary leash. Mike takes the flag to wipe his rifle clean, then goes inside the house to announce to Beth that Jake is waiting outside to apologize. Beth doesn't want to go outside. She prefers the safety and sheltering illusion of her four walls. After all, her husband-to-be Frankie, her promise of a future, is within these walls. Only the past trying to reclaim its presence is out there.

Mike's trouble is not only with Beth, on whose behalf he has given so much time and effort, but with his father. His father is very upset that Mike used an American flag as a dust wiper on a gun. He chews Mike out for his seeming lack of patriotic respect. Turning from his father, Mike leads Beth to Jake, who is standing on two legs now. Jake is no longer obeying Mike, but he does not make the protestation of love to Beth that he had promised himself he would make when he began his long journey. He knows the time has passed for that kind of connection. When Beth tells him that she is marrying his brother, Jake kisses her tenderly on the forehead, releasing her and thus releasing himself from his passion/obsession. He exits offstage into the darkness.

Mike has wanted some praise for all the work he has done: the beating of Jake, the winning of Jake's submissiveness, the care he has given his sister in speech and physical therapy, but no one is paying any attention to him. His father Baylor is more concerned with the blanket he wants to keep warm; the father steals the blanket from Frankie, who had stolen it from him. In angry reaction to the family's negative attitude, Mike leaves the house. Like Jake, he is making an exit and a statement.

The coda of *A Lie of the Mind* is one of Shepard's most tender pieces of writing, and certainly one of his most finished ones, both in thematic resolution and in polished style. Two brothers have left home—Mike has gone off alone, unable to understand his family: Jake has walked off, alone, perhaps understanding his wife and himself a little better and at the least accepting the finality of a failure of relationship. Left on stage are the mother and father: Meg and Baylor are folding the American flag Jake has left behind. They are doing something together: Meg is pleased to take Baylor's instructions on how to fold the flag because he is talking to her; they are involved. He has even kissed her on the forehead—Meg says it is the first time he has kissed her in twenty-five years. Having done a good night's work—the folding of the flag—Baylor tells his wife he's going to bed, and she says, happily, she'll be up soon. Bayor has not really changed, for he warns her not to come to bed and wake him in the middle of one of his good dreams: she is to keep her respectful distance. Yet the paradox is apparent: though there is a distance between them, tonight there has also been a bridge over that distance. Accepting the distance between them is the method of finding the bridge over those distances. Meg realizes this as she looks into a fire burning in a bucket on stage, which she compares to a fire burning in the snow. It is on this image that the play ends.

Snow for Meg, as it was for "Mom" in *Fourteen Hundred Thousand* is a beginning, it is a pure white canvas of a start, it is a magical world. It is the place in Meg's memory when the family is together because the show has locked them into its hulking hug. The roaring fire idealized in *Fourteen Hundred Thousand* is drawn from the same tone of warmth suggested by the family house in Montana in *A Lie of the Mind*. Whenever outside forces threaten to coerce a family, the family sticks together. For Meg, such a moment has come tonight: the family has been joined again. The magic still works. There is snow falling over Montana.

If Shepard sounds romantic at this point, he is not hopelessly so. He has made it clear that Meg is eccentric if not a bit wacky (her mother was put away in an institution, and Meg is awfully vague about everything), and Beth is a mental retard. Baylor is blind in his self-centeredness. Given these limitations, the family yet remains together, the family is operating as a family. Shepard's "family" lives in a place filled with limitations, but its values continue to nurture his spirit and to provide him with a landscape of his own.

8

Shepard's Picture of Illusion

What are illusions for, if not to help us see things through? Any reader, any theatergoer, any participant in life has been taught that illusion is a false reality, that it is a disease that afflicts the many but that must be kept in check if psychological health and stability are to be achieved. A Shepard character might say, "We have to use the mind to get by," and his statement would immediately be subject to ironies of Shepard's wit. For, in Shepard's view, the mind tells a lie when it orders inconstant material into a seeming flow of rational order. Such an attitude underpins Shepard's title *A Lie of the Mind,* for in that work the characters have rationalized their situation into a manner and mode of life they can utilize for their daily coping. The truth of concrete reality is too hard for them to bear, so the mind creates another kind of reality, a "lie," which becomes their sustaining life force. That sustaining life force is called an illusion by many overseers of literature, but to call it illusion and have done with it is a misreading, or a mis-seeing, of what Shepard is pondering. While it is true that the mind "lies" for the sake of its owner's contentment, the lie is not necessarily a falsity of reality nor a cancer of the soul. The "lie," or illusion, while not behavioristically verifiable, remains a potent source for psychic retention and regeneration. Shepard's view of the "lie" and his characters' addiction to illusion is thus an ambivalent one. He both satirizes illusionary addiction and praises that addiction for what it is worth: a balm, a placebo, a crutch, and, at times, the enriching world of a character's dream vision.

Clarifying Shepard's attitude to illusion or "lie of the mind" may be achieved in part by a comparison of the outlines of his attitude with those of eminent playwrights who have preceded him. The role of illusion has been played since the first drama was written, and creative writers as well as mystics, religious leaders, and seers, have resorted to it. In the modern age, and particularly the modernist and postmodernist period, illusion is everywhere, but its outline and form pose greater problems of apprehension than they once did. In Greek drama the distinction between "madness" and "reality" was clear. The "madness" may be divine or humanly corrupt, but there is no haziness about the times in which a character has slipped into a frenzy or a delusion. The onlookers' attitude to such leave-takings from common reality is distinct as well, even if the sympathies of one reader for a character divested of his senses may differ in intensity and range from another onlooker. Such a view of the divide between reality and illusion held pretty much intact from the Greeks through the twentieth century. Exceptions occur, of course; the work of the Marquis de Sade in the eighteenth century is a prominent example, and commentators on some Elizabethan playwrights suggest a shimmering of the lines between the mind's lies and the common weal. Christopher Marlowe's Dr. Faustus in this sense may be compared to a modern hero, and Lope de Vega's *Life Is But a Dream* suggests a surreal world of apprehension. Generally, however, and clearly in Shakespeare, the distinction between reality and leave-taking of it is abundantly clear. The pathos, in Shakespeare, comes from viewing man's fallen state in a commonly held reality.

With Ibsen, a door did not close on one kind of reality and open on another, but a different kind of consciousness emerged from underworlds kept hidden. Ibsen set out to battle human addiction to hypocrisy and venal compromise. In the process he chose as his weapon the exposure of corruption and greed, but such exposure could be seen only if the world about him of fraternal illusions were punctured. The illusions that some things were best left unsaid and unexplored became anathema to Ibsen. He created a storm of outrage in his bourgeois milieu by his clear portraits of opposing views and worlds of feeling. He ordered his view in terms of the distinction between self-interested illusion and naked selfless truth. In his mind, and in his age, the belief that truth could be apprehended once veils of illusion were shorn away still carried psychic force. Thus in *Ghosts,* Ibsen stripped away the illusion that a man from a distinguished family could not have syphilis, or that a mother could will away the tragedy of passing on a disease inflicted on her by a dissolute husband. In *An Enemy of the People,* he exposed the illusion that town counselors would honor the public concern of the townspeople in preference to their own greed and the amassing of personal wealth. In *The Wild Duck* he showed how illusions of self-centered egotism could destroy an unsuspecting family: goodness that knows no bounds or constraints for tolerance of other people's ways and alternative manners becomes a tyranny of benevolence. In *Hedda Gabler* Ibsen treated the illusion of a woman who believed she could control her world by the force of her will and that she could constantly keep it in the shape of a "beautiful" place of her mind; in her awareness of defeat by those she considered less worthy of high station she shot herself. In *A Doll's House* Ibsen stripped Nora of her illusion of accommodation: she, who had always appeased men, realized she must begin a new life. Her old world, shattered by the truth of exposure of the old lies of social prejudice, could not be rebuilt. When Nora closed the door on her "doll's house" and left her complacent husband, it was not to go to an easy (or easier) life but to a possibility of an honest one.

Ibsen's attitude to illusion then is a straightforward divide. Like a general on a field of battle, he reconstructs naturalistically his plans of attack. He knows his enemy, and while he is not a chauvinist nor a patriot of any order but his own vision, he is an informed man who has come to distinctive conclusions. He knows not only what illusions are, but where they "lie" and how they "lie." In his mind there is no blending, nor vagueness of boundary between reality and illusion: when any confusion sets in, it is Ibsen's view that a disease of the spirit has invaded the body-soul. Such a certitude distinguishes Ibsen from his twentieth-century followers, who saw in illusion not only a willful escape from social responsibility but a new kind of order and vision, a restorative to social health rather than a breakdown. Luigi Pirandello, Samuel Beckett, Bertolt Brecht, Edward Albee, the early work of Harold Pinter and some of the work of August Strindberg, and to a lesser extent, Elmer Rice, are playwrights who show illusion as a creator of reality and that such creations and re-creations are not to be taken prima facie as decadent forms. Pirandello also introduces the notion of the artist as an illusion, that is, that the characters he creates take over the work created and shape it to their ends; a playwright must follow their lead as a subject writer. Shepard will display this attitude in his work many years after Pirandello; the display will be in different modes but in a kindred spirit.

Another prominent instance of illusion as subject of (not to) reality may be seen in the work of Eugene O'Neill, who treated in his plays both naked illusion, in the form of obsession and delusion and alcoholic mania, and technical illusion, the manner of masks and "asides" of the subconscious voice alongside the conscious, real speech of his characters. O'Neill's immersion in illusion can be seen in such early work as *The Emperor Jones, Anna Christie,* and *"The*

Hairy Ape" through his midcareer successes, *Strange Interlude, All God's Chillun Got Wings,* "*Marco Millions,*" to his later masterpieces such as *Long Day's Journey into Night* and *The Iceman Cometh.* O'Neill's use of illusion distinguishes it from the representation of commonly held reality; it becomes a nurturing world in which those who enter it abandon all hope of coping with an outside societal world. The universe of illusion in which they reside thus sustains their defeat of self at the price of obliteration of self-esteem; in its place is a fantasy world of self-illusion, not subject to examination by rude forces of social and critical observation. In choosing to enter their self-contained world of illusion, they have, like Ibsen, closed the door on a world of hypocrisy and petty ambition, but, unlike Ibsen, O'Neill's characters can no longer hold out any hope of opening another door after the one they have closed. Their agony and their sense of completion grow out of their willing surrender to the haze of self-inflicted illusion: they go out on a limbo to un-meet their challenges.

Shepard differs from O'Neill in that his characters are rarely self-pitying or semiaware wrecks of circumstance and character. While Shepard's characters may suffer from alcoholism, they do not glorify their addiction or turn it into poetry. Not even Shepard's recurrent father figure, the lone man on the desert imbibing the painted sky, flinches from what alcoholism has done to him: he curses his cross rather than accepts or poeticizes it. Shepard is more likely to use food, and addiction to it, in the way that O'Neill uses alcohol. The most blatant example is *Curse of the Starving Class,* in which food, or the lack of it, is exemplified in the characters' hunger for a nourishing sustenance. Shepard's *Action* is another play in which the meaning of food is more important than the eating of it. Thus Shepard may be said to differ from O'Neill in his resort to illusion in that O'Neill makes poetry of an obsession and a weakness and Shepard utilizes imagery to signify a great wanting.

One other major American playwright with whom Shepard demands comparison in his use of illusion is Tennessee Williams. The two writers are worlds apart in mood, idiom, and dramatic structure, but they share common ground in their recognition of what myth, as turned into illusion, has done to American character. Williams is a preeminent delineator of Southern myth and of the defeatism engendered on Southern gentlemen and ladies by the dominating legends of the South. In all his work—plays, poetry, and fiction alike—his lens is on the vitiation of vitality in the milieu of the Southern aristocrat, and those who would ape him/her.

Whether man or woman, homosexual or heterosexual, the cynosure of Williams's portrait remains constant: in living up to impossible ideals, his protagonists fall down in defeat. The survivors in his work are those who do not push too hard, who accept imperfection, who recognize that a dream is a town to which they would like to travel but which they may not reach in their lifetime. The characters, however, whom Williams presents most lovingly are his soldiers of beauty, physical and cultural; such soldiers are defeated by the passing of time and their impossible demands on themselves. Yet they hold out the hope that through their beauty and their idealized vision, they can turn the world back into a better place; they are the soldiers of a chivalric tradition that exists in legend eternally and possibly never in history. They are the practitioners of a self-indulgence that on its best days reaches a site of beauty; such a site has a location only within the confines of their inner eyes. The most famous of these lost souls is Blanche DuBois, who uses illusion the way most people use paper towels. She washes her eyes in it, she sweeps her table of the day into it. In the 1950s and 1960s Williams was the most popular serious dramatist of his day, creating an attention to illusion that dominated American consciousness. Shepard, and the playwrights of the 1960s and 1970s, are in part a reaction to Williams's glorification of illusion, or at least loving sympathy with whitewashed Blanche characters. The crucial distinction between Williams and playwrights after him lies in Williams's manner of indulgence, a manner and mode that even as it signified defeat also signals a dying heroism in the modern age. What—and who—survives is a realistic commonplace in Williams's work: the beautiful dreamers are damned to defeat and to brutalization. In contrast, Shepard's characters are not defeated by the boots of outer reality, for their illusions literally turn the real world into their own conceived fables. By their manic monologues they signal to the audience that reality can be transformed. Whereas Williams's dreamers escape reality by moving into fantasy, Shepard's manic monologists revise reality into a shattering new world.

9

Concluding Notes, and Notes on Shepard and His Friends

Sam Shepard is a curious mix of the private and the public. Like Greta Garbo, he has cultivated an image of the loner, a mythic figure of silent strength: when he speaks, it is with the substance of a man who has chosen isolateness as a vantage point. Unlike Garbo, however, Shepard is a family man, one very much attuned to the concerns of family business and the needs and cries of his family. Perhaps *families* might be a better term, for Shepard, while rooting his family portraits in his own experiences, gives each portrait a different name and several new angles of allusion to ponder. Indeed, the conflict between the public and the private role is one of the pivotal concerns in Shepard's work as that work gains in length and breadth of maturity. While conflict may be seen in his earlier works under the surface bombast of individual character's declaration of defiance, it is not realized till Shepard attempts full-length dramatic work and attains resolution in his craft.

Like Garbo, Shepard is a publicist of his eccentricities, whether assumed for a public posture or whether such peculiarities are ineradicably substantial. As an apologist for the mystique of the lone cowboy—a strong man who can shovel shit for fourteen hours a day and still stand up tall before a bar in social conformity—Shepard exhibits a resoluteness and an evasiveness in his work and in his personality. The contradictions and the conflicts between desire for privacy and yearning for the companionship of spirited audience are elements that fuel his work and give it tension and excitement. In his extracurricular activities—both those having to do with publicity for theater and movie business and for the world of literary myth—Shepard has not only exhibited his contradictions, he has exploited them. He has on occasion given interviews, appeared publicly for screen shenanigans and hustled in the modish world of theater "events." On just as many occasions he has walked off sets, fled to his mountain or ranch retreats, and holed himself up with family, friends, and horses, cows, dogs, and a verifiable peaceable animal kingdom. Shepard once drove off to Vermont after giving an opening night performance in the lead role in his play *Cowboy Mouth;* the flight was provoked by Shepard's anxiety, both professionally and personally. Ironically, the reviews of both the play and Shepard's performance were favorable, but Shepard was unable, psychically or geographically, to make it back to the off-Broadway theater before the production closed for lack of its star hero. Shepard's real vulnerability may also be seen in his fictionalized autobiographic portrait of Slim in the play from which he ran away, *Cowboy Mouth,* and in several other plays, notably *Geography of a Horse Dreamer* and *Melodrama Play.* In these three works, Shepard's heroes are pursued by furies wanting a Messiah or a "winner." In *Cowboy Mouth* a street wench kidnaps the protagonist Slim because she wants to turn him into her Jesus rock star. That Slim (or Shepard) would like to help is apparent, but so, too, is his anger at the demands put upon him.

Shepard's protagonist in *Geography of a Horse Dreamer* is much like Slim in *Cowboy Mouth* in that he would like to please his audience, his parishioners, his family of man, but the protagonist in this drama is no longer a winner: he has lost his gift and skill at predicting the outcome of horse races. Shepard's fear of "losing it"—of the anxiety of the creative artist who wonders if his slipper of imagination will be empty the next morning—is evident in this work, as it is in *The Tooth of Crime,* a more naked portrait of a rock star exploited by his fantasies into his own victimization, and in many of his dramas from 1967 to 1980.

Shepard's friend Paul Pascurella describes Shepard's early work as "naturally unedited" pieces he "wrote from start to finish." In time, in Pascurella's words, Shepard came to realize "certain things can and certain things can't be done." Shepard himself has said that he now rewrites constantly before letting a piece out. Shepard has become a considerate writer of very considered judgments, a heavily self-edited craftsman. He not only rewrites his dialogue but his stage directions as well. Perhaps the greater significance lies in the revision of the directions, for Shepard is a playwright who very tellingly gives instructions on his characters in his accompanying commentary. His comments, for example, on characters' dress are insightful literary opinions beyond the manner and fashion of costuming; his directions on props and location are similarly phrased in imagistic, poetic language. It is interesting to speculate on this progression in Shepard's work. A case can be made that Shepard's considerateness and compassionate sympathy derive from his personal development as a human being. Certainly his early work is devoid of hesitation; its charm lies in its impregnable enthusiasm. When Shepard wrote his early plays—it may be more accurate to call them provocative scenes—he displayed a brio of a star performer. There is no apparent fear of failure in his presentation as well as no apparent fear of success; all Shepard seems to want is to play the game of drama and to enjoy the fruits and weeds of that playing. The first cracks of pain begin to appear in the satiric dramatization of his father's deterioration from a war hero to desert hobo and in the mother's surrender of hope.

Shepard's satire is sometimes savage, but more often it is affectionate, even teasingly tender in a young man's way. Always it is uproariously exposing. It may be compared at times to adolescent pranking on the weakness and vulnerability of adults. Shepard is hard on his adolescents as well as on his older characters, but he implies forgiveness of ignorance for the young. For the old he gives less shelter, though he takes them into his house of eccentrics. In his family plays he celebrates the strength of the mother and the dream-vision of his father. He is like D. H. Lawrence in this treatment of parents and also like Lawrence in his mystical view of love as a polarized force allowing for distinctiveness as well as union. In Lawrence's case, it was a physicality that attracted the real Mrs. Lawrence and the fictional Mrs. Morel of *Sons and Lovers* to her husband-to-be. Mr. Morel however never became more than a dreamer of a comfortable, warm house and an active pub life. In Shepard's case the physically vital and attractive father-husband had dreams and goals he could not dispense with and could not reach through some fate of circumstance or character. In both dramas—the real ones of Samuel Rogers and Mr. Lawrence and the fictional worlds of Shepard and Lawrence—the mothers stand by their husband while making known the depths of their sacrifice.

It is interesting to note that, in his relationships with his parents, Shepard dedicated *Seven Plays* (which contain the family plays) to his father in 1984, a year after the father's death; he dedicated *Motel Chronicles*, the story of his father's wanderings and Shepard's own journeys across the country told in the language of poetry, to his mother, the stabilizing force of the family, in 1982.

Shepard celebrates family loyalty as well in his depiction of brothers. In his early work the focus is on the conflict between father and son, with a woman (usually the mother) as the mediating figure. In his later work he turns to the relationship between brother and brother as his source of dramatic energy. Shepard did not have a real brother, but he has created several for himself in his dramatic works. (In *The War in Heaven* he and his collaborator, Joseph Chaikin, talk about the "partner in me"—the partner is the brother every man has within himself.) The brothers in Shepard's family plays are representations of differing but linked selves; each creates the possibility of bridging a divide, or healing a wound, while each becomes his brother's enemy or his rival. Though the rivalry between the brothers is apparent in *True West,* in which open hostility fuels the action, the brothers in *A Lie of the Mind* show more deeply Shepard's use of the sibling image as friend/lover and betrayer/destroyer. Shepard constructs two pairs of brothers as contrapuntal resonances of his theme: one of the pair (Frankie) goes to Montana to aid his brother's quest for knowledge of his murder of love; the brother in the other sibling relationship goes to a Los Angeles hospital to help nurse his sister back to health. Frankie wants to heal a situation by bringing the possibility of reconciliation to his brother's wife; he is in effect bringing a message in the process of confirming the right address. Mike wants to see his sister healed so that she can move away from her husband and return to the first family of her life's refuge.

The brothers, having done their job, must go off. They are, after all, agents of the imagination. When the imagining has been completed, their role is completed. Significantly, it is Jake, the husband, who must leave because imagination has proved him false to the situation; he no longer belongs in his wife's imagination. Mike, the more intelligent and belligerent of the two foils, does not walk off quietly as Jake does. He decries the ingratitude of his family.

Shepard usually writes more than one play on a subject in which he becomes interested. He does not collect notes in an orderly fashion although he is famous for collecting notes at seeming random, writing down dialogue on bits of paper and stuffing them in his shirt or pants pocket for some later ulterior purpose. Because of his work habits and because of his bias against sealed addresses to the public, he does put all of his notes into his plays in some coded way. Usually, some aspect remains submerged in the flood of his most compelling ideas, and, in time, this unnoticed or locked aspect springs up into being in a new play.

Shepard, also, has some concerns to which he returns in varying degrees of intensity. These concerns, themes, insights, illuminations, are part of the nexus of his vision. They are interconnected. His relationship with his father infiltrates all his work, a search that Shepard has conducted from *The Rock Garden* through *A Lie of the Mind.* Joyce Aaron has said that Shepard put all the older men he knew into his characterizations of the male, but that his father was the most important relationship of his life. Generalizations need qualification to have a modicum of intellectual force, but general patterns can be grasped. Such journeys invest Shepard's work not with psychological nostrums but with a texture and density of imagery that accretes into a truth grasped.

If I have likened Shepard to Greta Garbo, I should add that many see in his mania, or megalomania, for privacy a likening to Howard Hughes. Shepard's interest in Hughes as exemplified in *Seduced* suggests that Shepard may see something of himself expressed expressionistically in that legendary figure. Other critics have sometimes likened Shepard to J. D. Salinger and/or Thomas Pynchon, though, unlike them, Shepard is no recluse. Shepard's desire for privacy is understandable in the context of the demands of his public persona, but I wonder if at times he is not making much of a good (or bad) thing. Shepard has many friends, and some detractors; his friends have rallied round him to "protect" him. In the course of writing this book over a three-year period, I attempted to interview Shepard and his friends. I was unsuccessful in making contact with him. I did speak to some of his friends in Santa Fe and Taos, New Mexico, and in New York City. Each—both the kind and the rude ones—took the stance that Shepard would not want them to talk about him. Some expressed the view that Shepard needed to be "protected." Joyce Aaron—who agreed to see me in New York after she investigated my credentials and after she made it known that she was to be free to answer only questions she wished to answer about "Sam"—said Shepard was a delicate talent who needed his friends' support. Rosalie Murphy, the owner of the Pink Adobe Restaurant in Santa Fe, admitted that "Sam is a wonderful person, but a private one." David Winn, a polo-playing friend of Shepard, was gracious, but he carefully guarded his remarks, though he admitted that Shepard's attitude about privacy was "antediluvian." Paul Pascurella, a painter in Taos and a roper friend of Shepard, consented to a meeting and showed he could relax with an "outsider" (e.g., a professor from the East), but Pascurella reined in his remarks to painting and cowboy roping.

I print below some of the comments I was able to obtain about Shepard from his friends in New Mexico; all of them are protecting "Sam's" privacy.

Paul Pascurella met Shepard about ten years ago in Cibarron, New Mexico. Both men were ropers, trying out for prizes on the weekend rodeo circuit. They became friends, and Shepard has bought some of Pascurella's paintings. Like Shepard, Pascurella's work is informed by the Western mystique and by bold strokes: Pascurella's canvases are huge and confrontational. Pascurella says Shepard has never stopped being a cowboy—he dresses like one, although, in Pascurella's words, Shepard is no longer so lean and Gary Cooper–like. "I mean, he looks substantial now."

Another of Shepard's friends, the screenwriter David Winn, met him on the polo fields. Shepard began playing Indian polo and cowboy polo, but he is now a member of a traditional polo team and has a rating with the US Polo Association. (Winn says Shepard's rating is a high one.) The image of the anarchist Shepard playing in a game most often imaged as a memento of the British Empire is initially startling, but apparently Shepard is a good team polo player as well as an individualist in other matters.

Winn says that Shepard moved to Virginia in 1988 "because he always wanted to raise horses, and it's easier in Virginia, where there's grass." Both Shepard and "Jessie," Winn said, "wanted a farm in Virginia. The kids wanted horses, and it was also closer to New York than Santa Fe, while still far enough away from it." Yet, Winn said, Shepard misses the ambience of New Mexico, the sense of camaraderie rooted in Western legend. Shepard misses also his friends who are not professionals, not in the same business of writing as he, but with whom he can "talk." Unlike another friend in Santa Fe, Rosalie Murphy, who claims Shepard left New Mexico because the tourists were gawking at the front door on his lawn, Winn says Santa Fe was conducive to Shepard's work. His ranch was "isolated"; he could work without distraction.

William Smart, the director of Virginia Center for the Creative Arts in Sweetbriar, sent a response to my query. Shepard now lives in Orange County, Virginia, near the VCCA artists colony. Smart wrote on January 29, 1991: "I've not met him, but I've been to his house several times and know his wife. . . . At Halloween Sam built a big bonfire for the kids, and the next day he went off to buy 8 or 10 cattle. He's got about a dozen horses and plays the cowboy-farmer."

Each man is seen differently by his friends, though all may see a common streak in him. Some of Shepard's friends say Shepard does not like to talk "art" or "writing business." Winn says that Shepard misses such professional indulgence and stimulation. Certainly Shepard talks of theater with his longtime friend and associate, Joseph Chaikin, whom he visits periodically in New York. Chaikin, who has been suffering from ill health for several years, and Shepard talk of many things—friendship is after all more than professionalism—but dramatic enterprise is not ruled out of their conversation. Shepard then should be seen not as a primitivist decrying craft but as a craftsman fearing affectation.

If Shepard has his loyal friends, he also has his critics. Rochelle Owens, the author of *Futz, The String Game, Istanboul, Beclch, He Wants Shih!,* and *The Karl Marx Play,* was often cited with Shepard for their dazzling provocations of ideas and language, during the 1960s and 1970s. She wrote thusly about him in response to a letter from me (her letter is printed with her permission):

> Less a prince and more a princess was what occurred to me when I saw Sam Shepard. His facial skin looked soft, his thin body and passive eyes resembled those of Gary Cooper, but not of the Hollywood frontier, more of the American suburban mall. He was well-liked, he aroused caring concern in people for his well-being. They liked giving Sam things. Like Blake's angel. During the sixties at the beginning of his career, a devoted actress friend always made sure that she carried several copies of Sam's play scripts in order to be able to deliver them personally to strategic places: offices of theatrical producers, directors, backers, etc. With her subservient psychology and taste for the androgyn look in males, Sam was perfect, and he had the very best agent that an eager and ambitious young playwright could ever want and he didn't have to give her 10%. The faithful actress doted on him like a German shepard [*sic*]. But they separated and Sam soon married a pretty young actress, and yet he still would consult with his former woman friend about business matters and domestic problems. It seemed part of his character to involve people in his wonderful life. He was pleasing to look at and gifted as well. A *Village Voice* drama critic had fallen in love with Sam in those early years, and he always voted for Sam to receive Obie Awards. It was said that Sam Shepard was one of the very few heterosexual male playwrights in the avant-garde theatre. And a few heterophobic male playwrights coveted him, but mostly he drew everyone's affection and admiration.
>
> You search and search and suddenly you arrive upon the concept of a full-blown Anglo-Saxon messiah of the American theatre. A lucky one. He'll go straight to Hollywood.

Compare some of Shepard's contadictions. A friend of his said Shepard turned down a million-dollar offer to do a commercial that would be shown only in Japan. Such was Shepard's sense of integrity. Yet in the May 28, 1990, issue of *New York* magazine it was reported that Shepard would get a percentage of the receipts from a new restaurant, "Paris, Texas," to open in the Soho area. All Shepard supposedly would have to do would be "to hang out" there when he was in New York. What is the difference between a television commercial of a few minutes duration and an appearance in the flesh in a restaurant-nightery, both of which are paid exploitation? Perhaps Shepard needed the money in 1990 and not in the year when Japan beckoned (though Shepard is reported to have made three films in 1990, and the earnings from those ventures must have been considerable). Perhaps Shepard enjoys hanging out in a bar that is named after the movie for which he wrote the film script. Perhaps Shepard thinks he is promoting Western culture by drawing crowds to the Paris, Texas Restaurant. Whatever the reasons, it is an oddity that a paragon of the cowboy myth should stoop to payment for drinks. Buffalo Bill and Annie Oakley did the same thing, as did Sitting Bull, but only in their decline.

Shepard is as fine a poet as he is a playwright. He began writing as a poet and has continued to write poetry in his plays as well as in his songs and his prose pieces. His two books of prose and poetry memoirs, *Hawk Moon* (1979) and *Motel Chronicles* (1982), turn on the same experience as the plays. One can find counterparts of the plays in the poetic units in the two books. One of Shepard's poems ends with a revelation of why he thought a person he came upon in a restaurant was crazy: the man in question was not hiding "his desperate estrangement from people." Only in admitting our eccentricity, Shepard seems to be saying, do we regain our sanity and the essence of our humanism.

Shepard's work is in reverse order from other writers, who usually begin their careers with a lesser certainty of style, then develop into more textured and experimental forms of assured craft. Like other writers, Shepard works from the inchoate to the honed, but his early work is presented as a certain kind of unified vision. The later vision, the more accessible one, is another piece of work formed out of the same materials as the early work but ordered by the playwright's craft. James Joyce worked the opposite way, from the realistic to the wildly experimental, from the seeming presentation of brevity to the unending complexity of language as insight into the human soul. In Shepard's career the experiment with language comes first, is part of his seemingly cockeyed visions, and then the language becomes more prosaic, more conventionally shaded. The plays gain in depth but lose in the imagination of things as the most awesome of human experience; in his later plays the experience itself takes on equal due with the imagination of it. Experimentalism becomes shaped into delineated angles of realism, and psychological character—once scorned—becomes the key to understanding.

Political analysts sometimes divide the world up into "have" and "have-nots." Observers of morality often use the divides of "good and evil." Drama analysts prefer camps defined by a frame of interest. Some critics for example are more concerned with the resolution of a dramatic conflict than in the presentation and/or illumination of it. Others prefer the framing of the situation to any further speculative development. They remember the problematics as the source of their fascination. Their fascination weakens any resolve to put a contrived, a *made* solution to it.

Each side thinks he/she has a handle on the essential emphasis of the dramatic material. For one, solution or resolution is what drama has to move to, otherwise why start with a dramatic situation? For the other, resolution is of less importance, since the essential point of drama is a presentation of a situation for provocation of thought and reaction. I often cannot remember the endings of plays, while I always remember the premise with which they began. Thus clearly I am in the camp of drama as premise. Shepard, it seems to me, is also primarily interested in drama as an opening into a situation rather than a closing off by resolution. As he said to Michiko Kakutano, in the *New York Times* ("Myths, Dreams, Realities—Sam Shepard's America," January 29, 1984), "I never know when to end a play. I'd just as soon not end anything. But you have to stop at some point just to let people out of the theater. A resolution isn't an ending; it's a strangulation." Shepard calls himself the "ultimate foe of terminal stasis."

Shepard, I think, would like a book about his work to end on this note of a beginning.

Appendix

Sam Shepard's first-produced play in six years, *States of Shock*, began performances at The American Place Theatre on April 30, 1991, for what was described as a "world premiere." Originally scheduled to give four preview performances and to open officially on May 1 for a "limited run," the play was variously reported as "opening" on different dates. The procedure is not unlike that followed by Shepard and his producers in earlier plays: it allows for public reaction without prior notice by reviewers.

I attended the April 30 and the May 1 performances. During the April 30 performance a woman next to me said "It's different from the Sam Shepard I've seen." When I asked her if she meant this play was more serious than the others, she replied, "No. Weirder." Before the play began its May 1 performance, another young woman said, apologetically, to her modishly dressed mother, "You know it's going to be radical," to which the mother replied, "Of course. I can't wait."

The truth about the play is simpler. It is familiar territory in which the rites of charge and counter-charge, and the monologues of self-justification reflect a plowing of the ground Shepard has walked on before. Yet there are differences. For the first time, Shepard's father is given center stage and all other characters revolve around him. In Shepard's earlier work the father was at the core of the drama, but the father's role was subordinate to the son's leading character. Here the father is the protagonist and the son is his foil. It is as if Shakespeare had written a complementary drama to *Hamlet* with Claudius as the central character. Indeed, the ending of *States of Shock* is reminiscent of Shakespeare's tragedy in that the son kills his father after the father has engaged in what amounts, for him, to a prayer—that is, a plea for understanding and a declaration that he will acknowledge his crime of family desertion as well as accept as his son the young man whose crippled state he despises.

States of Shock is a short drama: it runs one-and-a-half hours without intermission. It thus harks back to Shepard's earlier work. The theme is nostalgia—in this case, the father who finally admits to his desire to bring back a world typified by the small-town certainties in the lyrics of "Goodnight, Irene." The father wants order, discipline, patriotism, and a white middle-classdom. He has no conception of his insularity, although, in one monologue, he reveals his knowledge (and glorification) of his isolation. He says that he has always been a man of isolation, one who has kept "his back to the mountain." Shepard and his director, Bill Hart, have dressed the father as a military man of all ages—when he first appears he is wearing a Civil War officer's frock coat, sword, and cap. He will remove the coat to show his jungle camouflage pants, a Gulf War style T-shirt. His boots are World War II paratroopers' issue; he wears World War I leggings. He has a tattoo that could come from any war. As played superbly by John Malkovich, he is a quietly seething body of physical strength.

The drama is set in a "family restaurant," at one point indentified as the all-American chain, Denny's. The Civil War colonel wheels in a paraplegic, who has long hair parted in the middle and wears black jeans and sweatshirt: he evokes an image of the displaced and dressed-down Vietnam veteran. As in some previous plays he bears a physical resemblance to the young Shepard (Michael Wincott, who plays the crippled Stubbs, is imitating, I think, some of Shepard's filmic gestures). The intent seems clear: the young man is a Shepardlike hero in conflict with the demands of a military-minded father. The father denies the cripple is his son. He says the young man is a friend whose "middle," or 80 percent of his body, was blown away by artillery; the blast went through the young man and killed the father's child standing behind him. The play thus becomes an open cry of loss as experienced in a young man's awareness of his father's profound self-centeredness and in the denials and tentative acceptance of paternity by the father. At the end of the play the son will kill the father just as the father had killed the son's life. Pointedly, the killing takes place as the father admits to the possibility of his errors.

Parricide is not a new element in Shepard's work, but in this play there are few surprises about it. The inevitability of the ritual murder lacks dramatic conviction precisely because Shepard is single-minded in his thematic presentation of it. His style is almost stately, and revelations are given so earnestly that the drama at times performs like psychodrama. The result is a drama less poetically charged and less evident in imaginative humor than any earlier Shepard work.

Three other characters, as well as two drummers behind a scrim screen in which battle action is suggested by multimedia effects, inhabit the stage. One is a waitress who loves the "menu" of the family restaurant. She tells the audience she was studying the menu "when the missiles fell." She misses the Cold War because political, social, and thus personal lines were clearly drawn then; she knew who the "enemy" was. The references to the "enemy' are a reinforcement of the bond that holds father and son together. In the son's childhood they shared a common enemy, for the father dictated such knowledge and the son acquiesced as a testament of love and honor to the father. As the son grew older, he and the father became their own enemies, and this knowledge became a bond of affection between them, for as long as they opposed each other they shared each other. When the identity of the enemy becomes clouded with doubt, the father and son must go their separate ways. Perversely, the son blames the father for his own awareness of the father's limitations: the fallen idol becomes a betrayer of the acolyte's dream.

Shepard's handling of the theme does have power. The "son's" refrain lines, "I remember the day you forsake me" and "You invented my death," evoke the never-ending agony of psychic destruction. The father's whipping of the wounded paraplegic lying helpless on the restaurant floor shows a horrifying but dynamic resort to violence that Shepard has not appropriated before. In his earlier work Shepard used lyric violence, or the whipping of words, as his means of characterization. In this play there is less manic monologue and more conventional realism. Shepard, for example, has his impotent young hero yearn to "get back his thing," and at one point the paraplegic cries out in standing elation, "My thing's come back." For Shepard, to resort to such easy dramatic resolution and such banal language is a disappointment, and yet in spite of these literary impotencies the power of the play works a magic. Its wounding cry rankles attention.

Shepard uses a middle-aged-white-middle-class couple as his ironic choral comment on the state of America. Here again the viewpoint is a familiar one. Shepard has consistently blamed middle-class values of status and convention for their etiology of youthful vitality and experimentation. The condescending and intolerantly comfortable retirees—both husband and wife are dressed entirely in white sports clothes as they sit in the coffee shop—bear the brunt of Shepard's fiercest satire, and they have the penultimate lines. The husband sings "Goodnight, Irene" as a tribute to those values by which they have lived, a state of life that now exists only in the cocoon of their mind and in the barricaded confines of the "family restaurant." It is however the father, who has been killed and who revives briefly, who has the last line. Ironic and perverse, the father sings a chorus of "Goodnight, Irene," changing one line to announce his threat to take morphine if he does not get his way with the Irenes of today.

What strikes the viewer of Shepard's new play is his obsessional link with the memory of his father. The "wound" has always been a source of power for the artist, and Shepard is clearly an artist who has turned biographical injuries into art. That his family memories continue to provoke powerful drama is good news, but some concern may be voiced in Shepard's reversion to a lack of individual women characters. The two women on stage are, as in the early and middle work, one-dimensional foils for the male characters. The new work—if it is new work (I do not know if the play is a revision of an earlier script or one written during the past six years)—is thus not a moving-forward for Shepard. It is a *stasis* that continues, for the moment, to generate an urge for tragic art.

Bibliography

Collections of Plays

Five Plays. Indianapolis: Bobbs-Merrill, 1967 (*Chicago; Icarus's Mother; Fourteen Hundred Thousand; Red Cross; Melodrama Play*). Repr., Urizen Books, later Applause Theatre Book Publishers, New York, 1981.

"The Unseen Hand" and Other Plays. Indianapolis: Bobbs-Merrill, 1971 (*The Unseen Hand; 4-H Club; Shaved Splits; Forensic and the Navigators; The Holy Ghostly; Back Bog Beast Bait*).

"Mad Dog Blues" and Other Plays. Introduction by Michael McClure. New York: Winter House, 1972 (*The Rock Garden; Mad Dog Blues; Cowboys No. 2; Cowboy Mouth; Blue Bitch; Nightwalk*).

"The Tooth of Crime" and "Geography of a Horse Dreamer." New York: Grove Press, 1974.

"Action" and "The Unseen Hand." London: Faber, 1975.

"Angel City," "Curse of the Starving Class," and Other Plays. Introduction by Jack Gelber. New York: Urizen Books, 1976 (*Killer's Head; Mad Dog Blues; Cowboy Mouth; The Rock Garden; Cowboys No. 2*).

"Buried Child" and "Seduced" and "Suicide in B♭." New York: Urizen Books, 1979.

Four Two-Act Plays. New York: Urizen Books, later Applause Theatre Book Publishers, 1980 (*La Turista; The Tooth of Crime; Geography of a Horse Dreamer; Operation Sidewinder*).

Seven Plays. Introduction by Richard Gilman. New York: Bantam Books, 1981 (*Buried Child; Curse of the Starving Class; The Tooth of Crime; La Turista; True West; Tongues; Savage/Love*).

"Fool for Love" and "The Sad Lament of Pecos Bill on the Eve of Killing His Wife." San Francisco: City Lights Press, 1983.

"Fool for Love" and Other Plays. Introduction by Ross Wetzsteon. New York: Bantam Books, 1984 (*Angel City; Geography of a Horse Dreamer; Action; Cowboy Mouth; Melodrama Play; Seduced; Suicide in B♭*).

"The Unseen Hand" and Other Plays. Introduction by Sam Shepard. New York: Bantam Books, 1986 (*The Rock Garden; Chicago; Icarus's Mother; 4-H Club; Fourteen Hundred Thousand; Red Cross; Cowboys No. 2; Forensic and the Navigators; The Holy Ghostly; Operation Sidewinder; Mad Dog Blues; Back Bog Beast Bait; Killer's Head*).

"A Lie of the Mind" and "The War in Heaven." New York: New American Library, 1987.

Nondramatic Work

Books

Hawk Moon: A Book of Short Stories, Poems, and Monologues. Los Angeles: Black Sparrow Press, 1973. Repr., New York: Performing Arts Journal Publications, 1981.

Rolling Thunder Logbook. New York: Viking Press, 1977.

Motel Chronicles. With photographs by Johnny Dark. San Francisco: City Lights Press, 1982.

(with Wim Wenders). *Paris, Texas.* Ed. Chris Sievernich. Berlin: Road Movies; Nordlinger: Greno, 1984.

(with Joseph Chaikin). *Joseph Chaikin and Sam Shepard: Letters and Texts: 1972–1984.* Ed. Barry Daniels. New York: New American Library, 1989.

Select Uncollected Pieces

"Autobiography." *News of the American Place Theater* (April 1971).

"American Experimental Theatre Then and Now," *Performing Arts Journal* II, no. 2 (Fall 1977). Reprinted in Marranca, *American Dreams.*

"Language, Visualization, and the Inner Library," *Drama Review* XXI, no. 4 (December 1977).

Select Interviews

(in chronological order)

Gussow, Mel. "Sam Shepard: Writer on the Way Up." *New York Times,* November 12, 1969, p. 42.

Chubb, Kenneth, and editors of *Theatre Quarterly.* "Metaphors, Mad Dogs, and Old Time Cowboys." *Theatre Quarterly* IV, 15 (August–October 1974): 3–16. Reprinted in Marranca, *American Dreams.*

Coe, Robert. "Saga of Sam Shepard." *New York Times Magazine,* November 23, 1980, pp. 56ff.

Hamill, Pete. "The New American Hero," *New York,* December 5, 1983, pp. 75ff.

Kakutani, Michiko. "Myths, Dreams, Realities—Sam Shepard's America." *New York Times,* January 29, 1984, sec. 2, pp. 1, 26.

Boyd, Blanche McCrary. "The Natural." *American Film: Magazine of the Film and Television Arts* X, 1 (October 1984): 22–26. Also printed in *The Face* (London), no. 59 (March 1985).

Lippman, Amy. "An Interview with Playwright Sam Shepard." *Dialogue,*

April 1985, pp. 50, 58–59. Reprinted from *Harvard Advocate,* 1983.
Kroll, Jack. "Who's That Tall, Dark Stranger?" *Newsweek,* November 11, 1985, pp. 68–74.
Cott, Jonathan. "*The Rolling Stone* Interview: Sam Shepard," *Rolling Stone,* December 18, 1986, pp. 166ff.
Allen, Jennifer. "The Man on the High Horse," *Esquire,* November 1988, pp. 141ff.

Critical Sources

Books

Auerbach, Doris. *Sam Shepard, Arthur Kopit, and the Off-Broadway Theatre.* Boston: Twayne, 1982.
Bigsby, C. W. E. *A Critical Introduction to Twentieth Century American Drama.* Vol. 3, *Beyond Broadway.* Cambridge: Cambridge University Press, 1985, pp. 221–50.
Blumenthal, Eileen. *Joseph Chaikin.* Cambridge: Cambridge University Press, 1984.
Cohn, Ruby. *New American Dramatists 1960–1980.* New York: Grove Press, 1982.
Contemporary Authors. New Revision Series. Vol. XXII. Detroit: Gale Research Company, 1988.
Contemporary Literary Criticism. Vol. IV, 1975, Vol. VI, 1976, Vol. XVII, 1981, Vol. XXXIV, 1985, Vol. XLI, 1987. Detroit: Gale Research Company.
Dictionary of Literary Biography. Vol. VII, *Twentieth-Century American Dramatists.* Detroit: Gale Research Company, 1981.
Dugdale, John. *File on Shepard.* London: Methuen, 1989. Writer-Files series, gen. ed. Simon Trussler.
Hart, Lynda. *Sam Shepard's Metaphorical Stages.* Westport, Connecticut: Greenwood Press (Contributions in Drama and Theatre Studies, no. 22), 1987.
King, Kimball, ed. *Sam Shepard: A Casebook.* New York: Garland, 1982.
Lahr, John. *Up against the Fourth Wall: Essays on Modern Theater.* New York: Grove Press, 1968.
———. *Astonish Me.* New York: Viking, 1973.
Marranca, Bonnie, ed. *American Dreams: The Imagination of Sam Shepard.* New York: Performing Arts Journal Publications, 1981.
———, and Gautam Dasgupta. *American Playwrights: A Critical Survey.* New York: Drama Book Specialists Publishers, 1981.
Mottram, Ron. *Inner Landscapes: The Theater of Sam Shepard.* Columbia: University of Missouri Press, 1984.
Oumano, Ellen. *Sam Shepard: The Life and Work of an American Dreamer.* New York: St. Martins Press, 1986.

Patraka, Vivian, and Mark Siegel. *Sam Shepard.* Boise, Idaho: Boise State University Western Writers Series #69, 1985.

Poland, Albert, and Bruce Mailman. *The Off-Off-Broadway Book: The Plays, People, Theatre.* New York: Bobbs-Merrill, 1972.

Shewey, Don. *Sam Shepard: The Life, the Loves behind the Legend of a True American.* New York, Dell, 1985.

Sloman, Larry. *On the Road with Bob Dylan: Rolling with the Thunder.* New York: Bantam Books, 1978.

Smith, Patti. "Sam Shepard: Nine Random Years (7+2)" in Sam Shepard: *Mad Dog and Other Plays.*

Weales, Gerald. *The Jumping-off Place: American Drama in the 1960s.* New York: Macmillan, 1969.

Essays and Reviews

Bachman, Charles R. "Defusion of Menace in the Plays of Sam Shepard." *Modern Drama* XIX, 4 (December 1976): 405–15.

Bigsby, C. W. E., Kenneth Chubb, Malcolm Page. "Theatre Checklist Number Three: Sam Shepard." *Theatrefacts* 3 (August–October 1974): 3–11.

Blau, Herbert. "The American Dream in American Gothic: The plays of Sam Shepard and Adrienne Kennedy." *Modern Drama* XXVII, 4 (December 1984): 520–39.

Chubb, Kenneth. "Fruitful Difficulties of Directing Sam Shepard." *Theatre Quarterly* IV, 15 (August–October 1974): 17–25.

———. "Sam Shepard's London." *Canadian Theatre Review* 10 (Spring 1976): 119–22.

Demastes, William W. "Understanding Sam Shepard's Realism." *Comparative Drama* XXI, 3 (Fall 1987): 229–48.

Eder, Richard. "Sam Shepard's Obsession Is America." *New York Times,* March 4, 1979, sec. 2, p. 1.

Falk, Florence. "The Role of Performance in Sam Shepard's Plays." *Theatre Journal* XXXIII, 2 (May 1981): 182–92.

Freedman, Samuel. "Sam Shepard's Mythic Vision of the Family." *New York Times,* December 1, 1985, sec. 2, pp. 1, 20.

Jones, David. "Sam, Sam, Mythological Man." *London Review of Books,* May 2, 1985, pp. 21–27.

Kleb, William. "Sam Shepard's *Inacoma* at the Magic Theatre." *Theater* 9 (Fall 1977): 59–64.

Kramer, Mimi. "In Search of the Good Shepard." *New Criterion.* II, 2 (October 1983): 51–57.

Lion, John. "Rock and Roll Jesus with a Cowboy Mouth." *American Theatre,* April 1984, pp. 66–69.

Madden, David. "The Theatre of Assault: Four Off-Off-Broadway Plays," *Massachusetts Review* 8, no. 4 (1967): 713–25.

Mazzocco, Robert. "Heading for the Last Roundup." *New York Review of Books,* May 9, 1985, pp. 21–27.

Nightingale, Benedict. "Even Minimal Shepard Is Food for Thought." *New York Times,* May 9, 1985, sec. 2, pp. 5, 26.

Rosenblum, Ron. "Jessica Lange: Sex and Subtext." *Vanity Fair,* October 1988, pp. 142–43, 189–96.

Simon, John. "Soft Centers." *New York,* June 13, 1983, pp. 76–77.

Wetzsteon, Ross. "Sam Shepard: Escape Artist." *Partisan Review* 49, 2 (1982): 253–61.

Wilcox, Leonard. "Modernism vs. Postmodernism: Shepard's *The Tooth of Crime* and the Discourses of Popular Culture." *Modern Drama* XXX, 4 (December 1987): 560–73.

Wilson, Ann. "Fool of Desire: The Spectator to the Plays of Sam Shepard," *Modern Drama* XXX, 1 (March 1987): 560–73.

Index